Text design by Mary-Ann Zykin
Editorial production by Jocelyn Kerr

ISBN: 978-0-692-16474-7 (print), 978-0-692-16479-2 (ebook)

Distributed by IngramSpark

THE SIX-FIGURE BUSINESS BROKER

A STEP-BY-STEP GUIDE TO BROKERING SUCCESS

William M. Thomas

To my devoted wife, Aleyka, you have always been the wind beneath my wings.

Table of Contents

CHAPTER 1

Becoming a Business Broker

My mother said to me; "If you are a soldier, you will become a general. If you are a monk, you will become the pope." Instead, I was a painter and became Picasso. —Pablo Picasso

The Purpose of This Book

There are hundreds of books and courses on how to become a residential or commercial real estate agent, there are even a few books on the ins and outs of investment banking, but there are very few books on the market to assist new agents with becoming business brokers ("business broker" is a term used to describe both brokers and agents who handle small business sales and acquisitions). Prior to becoming a business broker myself, I was a pilot and flight instructor and eventually worked my way through law school and became an attorney that handled closings for business brokers. This combination of experience is what prompted me to create this how-to manual for new agents and for residential real estate agents interested to learn a new career.

As a closing attorney, my biggest frustration with business brokers was their lack of preparation. Lack of preparation leads to failed deals, and I'm sure they were frustrated as well. One of the worst situations I ever came across was when we were at the closing table and the seller mentioned that he closed his business four weeks prior and the brokers had no idea. This is just one extreme example where the two brokers involved did not do their job diligently. Perhaps the brokers would not have been able to keep the seller in business, but they certainly would have been able to save us all from wasting a month's time and work on a deal that would never happen. There are a lot of things that need to be dealt with ahead of time, so the buyer and seller are on the same page during the contract and at closing. A good business broker will investigate both the buyer's and seller's backgrounds, assist in arranging financing and credit, perform due diligence on the seller's business prior to listing it, and make sure that the buyer and seller have had a meeting of the minds prior to having them sign a purchase agreement. All of these things take time and effort on the part of the business broker; however, they must be done to avoid wasting everybody's time.

As a flight instructor, I've written FAA approved syllabi, taught a college course, and taught hundreds of students to fly—many of whom have gone on to fly with major airlines. Training was my forte for years prior to becoming an attorney. As a prior instructor, I know the easiest way for people to learn is to present information in as straightforward a way as possible: A little bit of theory followed by a step-by-step guide. This is as practical a guide for beginners as I could make it. As you're reading through this guide, I've added advanced tips and real-life experiences to set you on the right path.

What You'll Get From This Guide

- Step-by-step guidance through the business buying and selling process
- Checklists and insider tips for managing deals and different types of clients
- A forms section (at the end of the book) featuring templates and examples of commonly used documents
- Real-world examples and advice from the field

Traditionally, for a new business broker agent or a residential real estate agent wanting to learn to become a business broker, you needed to get hired by a business broker as an agent or become an assistant on a commission basis (for free) and then spend your time on the telephone looking for prospects. On the other hand, by using this book and training material, you can accelerate your learning curve, jump right in and start gaining clients and developing a network without the tedious and draining phone prospecting.

It always amazes me how some brokers have a complete disregard for a new agent's need to make money and survive. Prospecting will not make you a successful agent. Only by building a portfolio of listings and developing a network will you be able to compete and survive as a business broker. You need information, guides, and tools to be able to work as a business broker. I made the goal of this training program to provide you with all of those things. In fact, I promise you that after reading this book you will be able to start handling clients on your own. The book is written with the intention of teaching a person with no experience how to obtain clients, take listings, create deals, and make money as a business broker. This is done by giving you a cookie-cutter model. Each step in the model contains a full explanation of what you are doing and why you are doing it, so you don't just follow the model but obtain a deeper understanding of the entire process.

It has been said many times, in many ways, that if you truly understand something, you are able to state it so simply that anybody can understand it. It's my intention to create a simple path for you to follow from the first step in the process through closing a deal. You will be able to find clients and then counsel and lead them through the entire business sales process with confidence and professionalism.

Why Become a Business Broker?

The short answer is simple: because it is a rewarding and fun career with an unlimited earning potential, and for the most part, business brokers work regular business hours Monday through Friday and can set their own schedules with time off as needed. I regularly spend a week or more in the Bahamas or on the ski slopes each winter. Sure, I'll have to answer some emails or schedule some telephone calls while on vacation, but everything happens fairly slowly and there are rarely any fires that need to be put out at a moment's notice. The longer answer includes things like we have a great social network, we are happy to cooperate on listings, the business is intellectually stimulating and more attuned to solving a puzzle than to sales, and there is very little competition.

Interestingly, the job entails only a small amount of selling. Generally, this is because there is very little competition from other business brokers. Alternatively, if you decide to work as a Realtor, you will be competing with many other agents for the same listings. Of the hundreds of thousands of real estate agents in Florida, only about 2,000 are business brokers. It's not that the barriers to become a business broker are high or that the work is difficult, the reason is that it's been a well-kept secret. Many successful business brokers work by themselves or with only a few other agents. Brokers don't make big money by hiring agents and having them go get listings, they make big money by selling their own listings. This is a major difference between residential real estate offices and business brokerages. In the past, in order to break into the field, you would have to find a broker willing to train you. Alternatively, now that I've written this book, you can read on and learn enough to start on your own or convince a good business broker that you know enough to start working at their office.

If you want to list a business, you are more than likely going to get the listing because the seller isn't likely to know any other business brokers. The seller could find one by searching the internet, of course, but if you go and make a good presentation, it's not likely that the owner will call another broker. Even on the selling side of the transactions, you won't use a sales pitch for buyers, rather you will need to gain trust by mentoring your buyers, evaluating their situation and providing them with options and alternatives. Very simply, business brokers are deal makers who find opportunities to match qualified buyers with willing sellers.

In fact, for the most part, buyers and sellers are inexperienced at buying and selling businesses. The job of a broker is, therefore, to review and organize documents and financials for buyers, arrange financing, negotiate deals, and attend meetings with buyers and sellers to discuss the terms of the deals. The main skill necessary for business brokers is people skills: to be an effective communicator. Another good quality to have is to be organized, but don't worry if this is not your strong point, you can always hire staff and purchase software to supplement your lack of organizational skills.

Not only is a career as a business broker fun and rewarding but some agents will create a side business by investing in businesses and building a portfolio for themselves. As an agent, you will see the best and worst businesses for sale and you can see them before the public does. Investment opportunities may present themselves for you to invest in as you become experienced and knowledgeable with different business types. This may seem as an afar to what you are trying to accomplish at this point in time, but business brokers are problem solvers and deal makers—keeping an eye out for opportunities and making good deals are just intrinsic to the job.

If you are excited and ready to start, the next chapter is about getting set up to work as a business broker. It's important that when you start out and don't have a staff to assist you, that you take the time to get set up with communications, computers, and software. Things will get very busy very quickly and you will want to keep clients moving through the process without holding them back due to being overloaded with work.

Accelerated Learning Tip

In order to become a successful business broker, you have to first be a successful business broker: Start doing the things that successful business brokers do. Join business broker associations, take educational courses, talk to business buyers and sellers, and try to sell businesses. To do it any other way will simply take too long. Read this book and then jump right in.

Real-Life Experience

It was difficult to earn a good and consistent living during the first few years of business brokering. After about five years I had income, I had savings, I had some good investments, and I was glad that I stuck with it.

CHAPTER 2

Communications and Setup

If I had eight hours to chop down a tree, I'd spend six hours sharpening my ax. —Abraham Lincoln

Getting Setup to Work

In order to start working as a business broker it is crucial to develop the proper environment in order to service clients. This includes establishing memberships with organizations and online services, finding a location to work from, creating a website, starting an entity, establishing a business name, and possibly obtaining a state license. In Florida, as in many states, a real estate license is required for a third party to sell a business. Accordingly, I should also mention that in Florida a real estate salesperson is required to work under a real estate broker. For the most part, new business brokers start out as real estate agents (business broker agents) working under a real estate broker who specialized in business sales. The industry has developed terms for business broker agents to distinguish them from residential real estate agents. Agents generally refer to themselves as business brokers, business sales agents, business intermediaries, M&A Advisors, or acquisition specialists. For simplicity, I refer to new agents throughout the book as business brokers or agents.

Although some states do not have licensing requirements for business brokers, a real estate license is beneficial because of the inter-reliant work that exists between business and commercial real estate brokering. Commercial property needs to be leased or sold in conjunction with most businesses, and a business broker with a real estate license can handle both transactions. My agents are constantly using their real estate license to broker commercial property. Although they may only advertise business sales, commercial property sales and leases are consistently presenting opportunities and agents broker those deals just as easily as a business sale. Sometimes the commissions on leases can be very large. I've seen commercial lease commissions go into the six figures.

Also, most states have licensing laws that limit a real estate agent's ability to incorporate. If allowed at all, agents normally can only set up a limited liability company or corporation in their own name. Brokers, alternatively, can incorporate their brokerages in almost any name they want. Business brokers in unregulated states who do not need or wish to obtain a real estate license may incorporate their businesses as state laws allow.

Step-by-Step Guide

1. Check your state licensing requirements for business brokers. If there are any,

then you must comply. You should also consider getting a real estate license, whether it is required or not, so you don't miss out on possible commissions that come from selling buildings or leasing commercial space. Commercial sales go hand in hand with business brokering, so a real estate license is essential.

2. If a real estate license is required by state law, then it would be smart to find and apply for work with a real estate broker who specializes in business brokering. Getting hired by a broker that handles business sales will provide you with the environment and resources necessary to enhance your learning and jumpstart your sales.

3. Check around for business broker associations and multiple listing services that are region-specific to your area. There is normally one covering every locale, but if there isn't any in your area, you may join BizBuySell.com, Bizquest.com or IBBA.org (International Business Brokers Association). These sites and associations allow you to advertise your listings but also have valuable resources like educational courses and industry-specific documents.

4. A CRM (Contact Relationship Management) program is necessary to help you maintain and track contact information for buyers and sellers and allows you to track your deals. Microsoft Outlook is okay to start with, however, there are some nice choices that are customized to the real estate or business sales industry. Most brokers will provide this resource for their agents and some will even cover the cost for their agents. If not, you should pay the cost, knowing that a program will pay for itself by saving you time and helping you keep your clients and deals organized.

    •   Pick a program that is simple and convenient to use so you can spend your time selling rather than trying to figure out how to use or customize complicated software. There are many different programs that are customized for business brokers, but they can be expensive and difficult to figure out. I think it's much easier to use Microsoft Outlook or any other generic CRM instead. In fact, when you sign up to work with a broker, the brokerage may already have a CRM subscription for you to use.

    •   Most programs are cloud-based and come with smartphone apps so contact information and documents can be accessed from anywhere. These programs may seem costly at first, but you will find that the convenience will save time and allow you to work more efficiently.

5. If you don't already know how, you should learn to use a smartphone or a tablet. I know that sounds silly to the younger agents, but some of the more mature agents, born before the age of computers, can find these devices intimidating and frustrating. Having knowledge of portable devices and apps is important for doing business these days and you really can't get around it anymore. At

the very least, you should own and be able to work a smartphone, or else, you may have a tough time keeping up with clients and other agents. A lot of business is done from a smartphone and clients have come to expect it from agents in the industry. Texting is or will soon become the number one way that agents communicate with each other and with clients.

6. Access to a cloud-based storage service is very convenient and can be an important tool for agents. Most of these services offer free starter accounts or have a nominal fee to start. Smartphones and tablets don't hold a lot of data, so it may be necessary to store documents in the cloud, so they can be retrieved and forwarded from anywhere using a portable electronic device.

7. You should make business cards to hand out to business owners, buyers, accountants, attorneys, lenders, other brokers, and everybody else you network with.

8. Post cards or door hangers can be created to target sellers and posted on business entrances at night. I discuss this later in the marketing chapter of this book.

9. You should create a website to market both buyers and sellers. Again, more about this in the marketing section.

10. If at all possible, get an easy telephone number to remember. This may take a while, but with time, one should become available as there are new numbers available everyday as businesses constantly drop old numbers. I make use of this concept with the telephone numbers 561-BROKERS and 305-SUCCESS. All of these numbers are routed to an answering service, which forwards calls to the appropriate agent's cellphone. Some brokers use 800 numbers, but I found that customers want to know where they are calling and prefer to dial a local number.

11. You should set up an account with BizBuySell.com, Bizquest.com and possibly Loopnet.com (in that order) because they are the largest business sales websites and a have a high ranking on internet search engines. You will need an account to post listings and to search listings for your buyers. Loopnet.com is specifically a commercial real estate site but it can be used for posting businesses that also include real estate for sale. All three of those companies are owned by the same parent company but you must sign up for a separate account for each site. Furthermore, since retiring business owners sometimes own real estate for investment purposes, you can occasionally list their investment properties after you sell the business.

12. Create reasonable working hours for yourself. Generally, business and commercial agents work 9-5 Monday through Friday. A set schedule is an important tool for independently employed persons. This helps balance family life with work and promote a healthy attitude. That doesn't mean brokers can't work

in the evening or on weekends, it just means that brokers are expected to be working during regular business hours but will occasionally work after hours.

13. Although a membership with the local residential MLS may not be necessary, a membership with the commercial division of the MLS is wise for leasing or selling commercial real estate. Unfortunately, sometimes joining the commercial MLS requires you to have a membership with the residential Realtor's association as well.

    Alternatively, a membership with Loopnet.com or CoStar.com may be substituted for a membership with the local commercial MLS. Unfortunately, these memberships are very expensive, so it may be wise to postpone this service until it is absolutely necessary and start with a membership with the local commercial MLS. In the meantime, do the research and be ready to join Loopnet.com or CoStar.com at the moment it is needed (after you get your first commercial listing or buyer). Normally a membership can be set up in one or two days.

Accelerated Learning Tip

Take the time to become technologically organized while you are getting set up. Learn how to create a .pdf, send an e-signature document, set up an email account on a smartphone, and learn how to use the cloud to store and send documents. Young agents have no problem with these things. If you are going to try to compete with the younger generation, then you must get up to speed on these simple technical things that clients and other agent have come to expect from business brokers. Hire help if you need it, but don't disregard these necessities.

Real Life Experience

When I started, I wanted to find a grand name that sounded like I was the most experienced business broker in the world. I've been through a few different business names, and after more than 10 years, I finally figured out that sellers want to deal with me because they trust me. At the end of the day, they don't care what my business name is. If I had known what I know now, I would have named my business William M. Thomas, Business Broker.

CHAPTER 3

Documents

As a new agent starting out, it's important to familiarize yourself with the following list of documents. These documents come in many different forms with different language and different clauses. They may be purchased from a service or from an attorney in your state, however, for the most part, business brokers will supply copies of these forms or an equivalent to their agents. I've included copies of some of these forms in the forms section of this book.

Buyers Forms

1. **Buyer Tracking Form** – This form is especially useful to new agents for keeping track of buyers and their search criteria. Handling ten or more buyers at a time is hectic and this form will help keep track of the progress of each buyer. I use a spreadsheet and keep it electronically. You can do the same or print it out and keep a copy on your desk. If you are able to use a CRM, then that is even better. The problem I run into with CRMs is that when I get a reminder, I just dismiss it and then fail to get to the thing that I was reminded of. Having a list in front of me or on my computer screen is a constant reminder that this work needs to be completed.

2. **Non-Disclosure Agreement—NDA (also referred to as a Disclosure, Non-Circumvention Non- Disclosure NCND, or Confidentiality Agreement)** – Every buyer must sign a Non-Disclosure Agreement prior to receiving any information about a business or assets for sale. It is designed to protect sellers from unscrupulous or negligent buyers. It basically says that the buyer will not disclose confidential business information or the fact that the business is for sale to anybody (especially employees, customers, and competitors). One NDA should be signed by each buyer for each listing. In other words, use a separate form for each listing a buyer is interested in. There are many versions of this form. Generally, each brokerage or broker association has a form for its members to use. Many have clauses to protect the listing broker as well as the seller. The NCND form will also have a provision to protect the listing agent from third parties contacting the seller directly.

3. **Buyer's Profile Form** – This form is simply used to put the buyers contact information and the buyer's prior relative business experience in writing for the seller or seller's agent. It's a buyer's bio or resume, a snapshot of their background, especially their business experience. Aside from this form, it's perfectly acceptable to ask for a copy of a buyer's driver's license. Although it may seem like overkill, I've occasionally heard stories of sellers being scammed

with phony checks or competitors seeking information under false names. I personally don't ask for copies of buyers' drivers licenses, but if a buyer refuses to fill out the profile form, I won't proceed any further. Using this form helps provide organization, clarity and protection for sellers and agent as well.

4. **Buyer's Financial Statement** – This form is used to qualify a buyer financially. It is similar to a personal income statement that a bank would use to qualify a borrower for a loan. It's also okay to ask for proof of this information like a bank statement to go along with the form. I made a combined version of the Buyer's Profile Form with the Buyer's Financial Statement that I call the Business Buyer's Profile form. If you see the acronyms FP or POF, they are referring to the buyer's financial profile (FP) or looking for proof of funds (POF).

Listing Forms

1. **Listing Checklist** – Using a checklist when taking a listing is important because sellers need guidance. I use two different checklists, one for myself and another one I give to the sellers. Although sellers should be given a checklist, their version should be simple and only include the bare minimum. Don't overwhelm them with a long list of documents or you'll wind up with nothing. Start with a request for financials and a list of assets and then add more items in separate requests as you receive the documents from your previous request.

2. **Owner's Benefit Worksheet** - This form is used to adjust a company's profit and loss or tax return to show a more accurate representation of the bottom line. There are two versions of this form, one version for an individual tax year and a second version for posting multiple tax years on the same page for comparison purposes.

3. **Business Listing Worksheet** - This form is used during a listing appointment to write down the details that will later be used to create the listing. You can make this form yourself by reviewing all of the data necessary to enter a listing into your business MLS and make up a list of questions for your sellers to answer that will give you that information.

4. **Equipment List** – This is a list of assets and equipment that are included in the sale, along with an estimated market value for each item. You can use a spreadsheet to make this form for each of your listings. If the business also carries inventory, it can be included in a separate list on the same form. Including inventory here is only for a service business that carries inventory to complete jobs, not a business that is all inventory, like a grocery store.

5. **Listing Agreement** - The agreement between a business broker and a seller; whereby, the seller promises to pay a commission upon the broker bringing a buyer who is ready willing and able to purchase the business. There are

different types of listings, each requiring a different form. This is discussed in detail under the Sellers chapter of this book. Just like the NDA, this form comes in many versions and each broker or each association may use a slightly different version.

6. **Offering Memorandum (Memo), also called Confidential Business Review CBR, or a Confidential Information Memorandum CIM–** An offering memorandum is generated by the listing agent to provide buyers and their agents a summary of the listing (business for sale). For small businesses, it can be a one-page summary, but for large businesses, it should be very detailed. It is a report that should cover all of the specifics of the business for sale, like, financials, management, sales and marketing, employees, services or products provided, and assets.

Contract Forms

1. **Proposal or Letter of Intent (LOI)** - This form is simply a letter stating that the buyer has an interest in purchasing the business but would like to see if the seller will accommodate his offer. Normally, a LOI will contain one or more stipulations or requests; whereby, the buyer commits to buying the business, subject to the stipulations, at the price and terms stated in the letter. If the seller agrees, both parties would be prepared to go to contract upon all stipulations being met. Generally, this form is not an enforceable contract and agents will not earn a commission based on this form alone.

2. **Asset Purchase Agreement (Contract of Sale)** - The asset purchase agreement, or more simply referred to as the purchase agreement or contract, may initially start out signed by the buyer only; At this point, it is referred to as an offer to purchase. Once it is signed by the seller and a down payment is paid, then it becomes a binding contract. New agents always ask me how they make an offer. The asset purchase agreement is the form to use to make written offers. You may also use a LOI, but normally, for main street companies, the offer is written up on the asset purchase agreement which then becomes the formal contract after all parties have signed and the down payment is paid. Alternatively, a stock purchase agreement may be used for larger companies or more complicated transactions. This form should be completed by an attorney rather than a broker due to governmental restrictions on stock sales.

Accelerated Learning Tip

When you first start out, the lingo seems like alphabet soup: NDA, NCND, CBR, FP, CIM, LOI, IBBA, POF, CBI... The industry is full of acronyms that won't make any sense to you at first. Don't be afraid to ask questions. Remember that nobody starts out knowing what all of the terms and acronyms mean. We all had to learn them.

Real-Life Experience

I started out thinking that the business is all about having the right form for the right situation. And believe me, there are many different situations that require different forms. What I came to know however, is that the paperwork can be worked out prior to closing, but it's far more important to have a solid deal in place with a buyer and seller who are completely in agreement. If I don't have the right paperwork, then I just refer the deal to an attorney to draw up the necessary paperwork.

CHAPTER 4

Working with Buyers

I like to do all of the talking myself. It saves time and prevents arguments.—Oscar Wilde

Accelerated Learning Tip

Considering that the average business deal takes about six months to complete from listing to sale, new agents should start working with buyers rather than sellers. The reason being, a buyer can buy in a day and close in 30 days. That creates income that you can spend on marketing sellers. The other consideration is that a typical buyer doesn't know anything about buying a business and is not picky about who they work with, experienced or not.

Real-Life Experience

I hear agents all the time say, "Buyers are liars." Agents complain that buyers take them around to look at listing but never purchase any because in the end, they are not able to qualify for a loan or they never had the purchasing power they claimed. My thought is that these agents are lazy. If they had bothered to qualify their buyers in the first place, they would have notice the lack of purchasing power. Trust but verify. This allows you to work with only the good buyers. Work smart, not hard!

Take it Slow with Buyers

In order to become a great business broker, it's important to understand what your customers are buying. As Leo McGivena, the advertising genius, once said, "Last year one million quarter-inch drill bits were sold—not because people wanted quarter-inch drill bits but because they want quarter inch holes." And Charles Revson, the founder of Revlon said, "In the factory we make cosmetics. In the store we sell hope." To put this in perspective, business brokers sell financial freedom to buyers. They sell the opportunities to make large returns on their money, while staying in control of it. In the stock market as in real estate, an investor has very little control over the return on investment. As a business buyer, an investor has the opportunity to grow the business and increase the value tremendously, while maintaining control over the investment. This is the dream of financial freedom with control over their investment that buyers are seeking.

Business buyers are fairly easy to obtain because they are attracted to listings and advertisements. The fact is, the business sales market is not oversaturated with brokers with websites advertising the same listings over and over, like the real estate market is. The specific methods that brokers use to gain prospective buyers are discussed in the marketing section of this book. Now, let's talk about how to handle buyers. It is important to be diligent when working with buyers because statistically, only between five and ten percent of the buyers that you work with will close on a deal (the industry average for agents is one in 13 closings for buyers who they met in person and one in 36 buyers that they speak to on the telephone). I would imagine that this gets worse for buyers that are only contacted via email. This exemplifies the need for agents to create a relationship with buyers, but it also shows a need to work efficiently. Working with buyers is a numbers game: You will need to make a routine and stick to it; don't chase the big leads and neglect the small ones. Keep in mind that an agent with a 10percent closing rate will have double the closing rate as an agent with a 5percent rate. If you follow the procedure outlined in this book, then you should achieve a higher than average closing rate. On the other hand, chasing certain buyers and ignoring others will decrease your closing percentage and leave you frustrated. The idea of efficiency does not necessarily mean quickly: what I mean is that you have to direct buyers how you want to handle their search for listings. You need to get in front of them to find out what they really need, and to develop their trust in you. Without this, they will lead you around from one listing to the other and waste your time. If a buyer refuses to meet or comply with your requests, then move on to the next buyer. Remember, your focus initially with buyers is to get an in-person meeting with them prior to looking at any listings. This will give you a much greater chance of closing a deal with those buyers.

Even though it's not important to work with every buyer, it's a good idea to do just that when you start. It will give you experience at recognizing common buyer issues and how to handle those problems. As a buyer's agent (selling agent), you will need to be a problem solver. Most buyers don't know exactly what type of business they are looking for, and some have hurdles to clear prior to purchasing a business. Some of their issues include, the need for funding, an immigration attorney consultation, and lack of industry experience for the business they want to buy. Agents who take the time to listen to each buyer, and then counsel and educate them will find that their buyers appreciate the effort and return the favor with loyalty. This is another reason why in-person meetings are so important, so these issues can be discussed in advance, so you avoid wasting time doing unnecessary legwork. Agents who don't take the time to understand their buyers are susceptible to having their deals fall apart prior to closing. This is heartbreaking, frustrating, a waste of time, and totally preventable if you take the time to work your buyers diligently.

The First Key to Working with Buyers

When dealing with buyers, you should learn quickly to take the bull by the horns and lead buyers through the entire business purchase process. According to one study, about 90 percent of buyers are first time buyers, 90 percent of them will not buy the business that they call you about, and 50 percent of them will not buy the same type of business that they call you about. This statistic indicates that most buyers are sifting through listings on the internet and calling on the most intriguing ones. They really don't know what they want yet; therefore, it's important to get to know your buyers by first meeting with them and understanding their needs and their shortcomings. You don't want to show buyers the listings they request to see just because they request them. If they don't have the experience or the money to buy a certain listing, then it's not worth your time to show it to them. Sit down and have a conversation about what they need, and then try to explain why you feel those listings are not appropriate for their needs and why other listings are. Agents who learn how to do this for their buyers will be working efficiently and have a better closing percentage than other agents.

The Second Key to Working with Buyers

All buyers excel at one of three traits: sales, administration, or management. Of course, some buyers can be good at all three of them, but for the most part, buyers will exhibit one of the three traits as their dominant business trait. Knowing this will help you locate listings with an insufficient amount of the dominant trait exhibited by your buyer. These are the listings that will be the best fit for your buyers and your buyers will be willing to pay more for them than for other listings because they can see how the addition of the missing trait provides opportunity for growth for those businesses.

Let's say your buyer is strong in sales and he wants a dry cleaner business. You can't set this buyer up with dry cleaners that are lacking management because the first thing the buyer will think of is that he has to hire a manager to operate the business while he goes out and does sales. The salary for that manager will detract from the business profit and therefore, the business is worth less to that buyer than it would be to a buyer who is strong in management. On the other hand, if you show that same buyer a dry cleaner that has a great location but is failing because the owner does not market the business properly, the buyer will see great potential and ump at the opportunity to take over that business.

Working with First-Time Buyers

Let's take a look at a typical buyer and call her Mary. Now, let's say that Mary has $160,000 to invest, which is typical of what most buyers have to invest: between

$100,000 and $300,000. Mary, like most buyers, is looking to purchase a business between $300,000 and $600,000 and she wants an income of at least $100,000 per year. To do that, she will need to leverage her investment capital to purchase a business which is strong enough to generate her minimum income requirement. Many businesses can be purchased with a small amount down with financing for the balance. There are many ways to finance a business and as a business broker you should familiarize yourself with all of them. Buyers aren't usually aware that banks are willing to lend for business acquisitions or that sellers may be willing to hold a note to assist buyers with an acquisition. As a broker, you will have to introduce buyers to this idea and lead them through the process. Financing for buyers is discussed in more detail later in the book. Arranging financing should become an integral part of deal making for you. You will have to prequalify existing businesses for financing as well as prequalifying buyers for the purchase of a business. I explain how to do this in the chapter that follows.

Since most buyers are first-time buyers, you will need to educate them about the business purchase process. This includes introducing them to disclosures, financial statements, financing, and how to deal with sellers. Taking the time to explain the entire process and to guide them through it while not making them look foolish will generate appreciation and loyalty from your buyers. This can also create a bond of trust between you and the prospect. Trust is the most important variable necessary to bring a prospect from "just looking" to "making an offer." If a buyer doesn't trust you, it will be very difficult to make a deal. Trust is earned over time by walking buyers through the process and offering help at every step.

You should take the time to talk to buyers and ask them questions right from the start. Try to get to know your buyers' business backgrounds and what they want to accomplish in terms of their investment. It would be a good idea to recommend some possible listings or business categories that they may consider in order to learn about their particular interests. This will help you become an important part of the buying process. You should try to educate your buyers, rather than just a showing them listings and sending them information about listing being inquired about. Don't treat your buyers as a numbers game because you will continue to fail until you take the time to know what they need: educate them and give them the service that they are looking for. I can't emphasize how important this is for new agents to understand. Shot-gunning information to buyers will never work. You need to get to know your buyers, create a sense of trust, and create deals by leading them through the process and putting great effort into pairing them up with compatible businesses.

Going back to our buyer, Mary, the first thing you should ask Mary is why she is interested in buying a business. Perhaps Mary wants to use the purchase as an equity investment for some money she recently came into, she may want a second income, or she may want the business to replace her current job and use it as her first source of income. Getting to know Mary's motivations for buying a business will give you insight into which businesses will best suit her interests. Now, we know how much money Mary has, how much money she needs to make each year from a business, and her purpose for investing (either to buy herself a job, or as an investment). We still need to know about Mary's background. Knowing this will help us put the last piece of the puzzle together and be able to find her some good business prospects. Alternatively, if you just sent Mary a NDA in an email and asked her to sign it and send it back, you wouldn't even know how much money she has, never mind all of the other important criteria you need in order to sell her a business.

As you mature into a knowledgeable buyer's agent, you will develop an insight about how to select able-buyers and reject the tire kickers. This is nearly impossible to do as a new agent, but as you gain experience, you will develop a sense of which buyers are ready to purchase and which are toying with the idea of purchasing a business, or just don't have the money to buy a business. A really good buyer's agent will be able to weed out the buyers from the lookers and gain a higher than average closing rate. Be careful not to take the "fill out the forms or else I won't work with you" attitude, as that will alienate all of your buyers.

You must get information from prospective buyers in a tactful way during the initial conversation and then use your judgment to determine whether you want to work with those buyers or not. The best way to do this, I've found, is to strike up a conversation with buyers and start talking about all of the hurdles that you can help them clear. If you can do this at a face to face meeting, even better, but that isn't always possible because sometimes you only have one chance on the telephone. You can start by telling them that sellers get as many as 50 buyers looking at their business and this can be a great burden to sellers, especially since most buyers either don't have enough money to buy the business or are not genuinely interested in purchasing it: they are known in the industry as tire kickers. Then you can explain that you can prequalify the buyer to make them more attractive to sellers which gives them leverage when it's time to make a deal. Then you can explain your pre-qualification procedure and ask them if they would like your help. I'll discuss this process in detail a little bit later in the book. The important take here, is to strive to develop a sense for which buyers are ready and which are just looking in a short period of time or simply don't have the money to buy a business. Once you can do this, then you can keep the ready buyers and reject or refer out the others.

Working with Experienced Buyers

Experienced business buyers, on the other hand, are a world apart from typical first-time buyers and should be dealt with differently. They will call asking for information and details about a listing in rapid-fire fashion. They know what they are looking for in a business and if they don't get the information immediately, they will move on to the next agent in an effort to locate the actual listing agent. This may be overwhelming for new agents, but it only takes a few months of experience to learn how to provide these buyers with the proper information in a timely manner, which can lead to some very large deals. Experienced business buyers are often looking to acquire companies that are compatible with their existing company, so the businesses tend to be large operations with many customers or with a lot of assets. In the meantime, it's okay for you to slow down the conversation and tell these buyers that you are not the listing agent. There is not much else a new agent can do in this situation. It's important not to get caught up in the excitement and lie to these buyers. The truth will come out soon enough and both you and a buyer will have wasted time and effort. Normally, you should say that the listing is not yours, but you are keen at working for buyers and would be happy to help them in an expeditious manner. If they want to speak to the listing agent, then you can tell them that once you receive their signed disclosure and a buyer's profile form, then you will be happy to make the introduction to the seller or the seller's agent for them. That way, the buyer gets the information that he or she wants, and you won't lose your commission.

As with first-time buyers, experienced buyers must be prequalified if you are to work with them. In other words, until you know what your buyers' needs and financial abilities are, you will not be able to help that buyer. Even more so, when dealing with experienced buyers, the listings being sought are usually higher in price and of better quality; therefore, you will be dealing with sophisticated sellers and brokers who will want your buyers vetted prior to divulging information about those opportunities.

After the buyers have been interviewed and prequalified, whether they are experienced buyers or first-time buyers, the next step in the process is the information gathering phase. This entails gathering detailed information about a few qualifying listings for the buyer to review. Listing sheets only tell part of the story, there is usually more detailed information that can be obtained from the listing agent. This information is critical to buyers and the only way to get it is to telephone the listing agent and have a conversation about their listing. Most listing sheets make businesses look like perfect candidates, but in order to pick out the gems from the rocks, you need to investigate businesses before discussing them with your buyers. This entails calling the listing agents and getting the real story. The real story entails getting the true reason for the sale. This is the single most important factor for a buyer to know because it explains why the business is for sale. If a business is healthy and profitable, then why would somebody sell it? Did the seller run out of money? Is there a zoning or land-use issue? Is there a partnership problem? Is there a licensing problem? Whatever the reason is, you need to pick up the phone and contact every seller's agent in order to determine the real story for each of the listings for your buyers. The reason the company is being sold may qualify or disqualify a business for an individual buyer, but more importantly, it will enable your buyers to better set prices for these business in light of the risk or lack of risk that the reasons for sale project to your buyers. Contacting the listing agents also give you an opportunity to speak frankly with the agents and ask if your buyers are good fits for the business opportunities. Don't wait until you have gone back and forth between the buyer and seller with information and questions, ask upfront whether the agents see your buyers as good fits. This will save you countless hours of wasted time.

Investigating Listings for Your Buyers

As a general rule, listing agents will hold back business financials and memoranda of sale from published listings. Normally, when a business is offered for sale, the listing agent will make a spreadsheet showing the last three year's financials based on tax returns or profit and losses, and the same for the current year to date financial information. These are called the financials or financial report. Listing agents may also write up a report on the business indicating sales trends, management, methods of marketing, inventory, equipment, hiring practices, etc. The report is referred to as a memorandum of sale or memo. Listing agents will only release these reports to buyer's agents when they believe they have a qualified buyer. Financials and memos are necessary for evaluating the health of a business and understanding the specifics of how the seller runs the business. The best way to obtain copies of the reports is to call the listing agents and tell them you have good buyers. Emailing the listing agents may not always get you the same response as a phoning; therefore, I recommend that you call all listing agents to convince them that you have a good buyer and are requesting additional information including the financials and memo. The other reason to call is to find out if the business is under contract or getting close. If so, you may be wasting your time pursuing the opportunity and the best way to find out is by making an immediate phone call on each listing.

Once you receive the financials and the memo, you should call or meet with your buyer and review the information about the listing while trying to find positive reasons to buy it. Don't let your buyers make their own evaluation of each listing without first having all of the relevant information for the listings being reviewed. At first glance, buyers will notice that the asking prices do not always compare proportionately to the net earnings or sales figures. In other words, some listings look like they are priced too high and others look cheap. This will make buyers disregard listings that may be highly compatible and possibly nice targets for a buyer. You will need to slow buyers down at this point and ask them to give you time to gather information on each listing. Once all of the information is gathered, then the listings can be reviewed and compared to the others to weed out the worst of them and come up with a short list.

Seller's Pricing and Buyer's Valuation can be Divergent

Pricing a business is difficult and not always done properly by agents. In fact, the word properly may not be the right choice of word. It has been said that if a seller asks ten businesses broker to value his business, he will get ten different prices. There are just too many variables to consider when doing a valuation to obtain a constant single price; therefore, asking prices and offering prices can vary considerably. You should let your buyers know that it's normal to bargain with sellers and that average asking prices can be relatively high as compared to final selling prices. Buyers will need assistance with valuing businesses to help get a better idea of what a fair price might be. There is a tutorial later in this book to assist you with setting fair values on businesses. The main reason businesses are priced too high is that business prices are heavily based on intangible assets and future expected earnings which are not easily quantified. For obvious reasons, sellers set their values much higher than buyers, hence, the large spread between business asking prices and selling prices. Likewise, sellers and buyers perceive risk differently. Sellers are so comfortable with their business and their ability, that they don't see the risk that future earnings may decrease. On the other hand, that is all that buyers are worried about. Buyer's evaluate each business in terms of the risk of a decrease in future earnings and their offer price will go up or down based on the risk they perceive. The more risk buyers perceive, the lower the price they will be willing to pay.

Petition Offers from Buyers as Often as Possible

Don't expect to coax buyers into purchasing overpriced businesses, however, you should be able to solicit an offer for all of the businesses that seem to be a good fit your buyers. If your buyers are walking away from good opportunities, then you are doing something wrong or you are working with buyers who are not serious or ready to buy. If a buyer is interested in a particularly good business, it's important to be slightly assertive and encouraging that it is time to move forward with an offer, so the opportunity is not missed. For example, if our fictitious buyer Mary was interested in a well-priced dry-cleaning store after looking at several others, I would be sure to mention to Mary that she is unlikely to find another similar deal because deals like this only come along once every few months or even every few years. I would recommend to Mary that she should put in an offer right away, so we can start due diligence on the business. I'd explain to Mary that she would only have to put a small down payment in escrow and that money is refundable if she decides not to purchase the business. By advising Mary to make an offer, I am being assertive, but by explaining the process and letting her know she is not locked in, I am also encouraging her to make the offer. At the same time, if Mary doesn't make an offer, you should consider whether to continue working with her unless she has a good reason for forgoing the listing. Perhaps Mary is really a tire kicker and not a good buyer—this will be for you to decide when you have a Mary.

Business brokering is a numbers game: the more offers you can generate, the more deals you will close. Convincing buyers that they need to put in the offer and make the deal takes practice and experience and is something you need to work at. Sometimes this is easy, as buyers will fall in love with a listing and they will tell you that they want the business; however, most buyers will need some encouragement and prodding. If they like a business and are interested, but are having second thoughts, you will need to find out what the specific issue is, so you can solve the problem for them. A talented agent will get to know the issue and find a way to get the buyer past it. Sometimes, you can use price as a way to fix things. Sometimes you can use seller financing as the fix. There are a multitude of ways to fix issues, but you need to learn to do this so as not to miss out on sales. Again, you don't want to prod a buyer into a bad deal but remember that there is no perfect deal. Every business will have some fault to it but if it's a good fit for the buyer and the buyer can overcome the faults, then you should be able to get your buyer to make an offer.

When buyers show particular interest in a listing, it probably means they like what they see and want to make an offer. That's where you come in. Gather up all of the listing information, so you can start a valuation for them. If your valuation comes in much lower than the asking price, don't panic. Call the listing agent and ask why the asking price is so high. Discuss your valuation with the listing agent and ask if it would offend the seller if you come in with a low offer. This is a polite way of asking whether they will consider low offers. Here is a little tip, don't call low offers lowball offers, call them fair or reasonable offers. Linguistics may not seem important but lowball has a negative connotation to it and buyers may think that if you are trying to cheat the seller then you may also try to cheat me.

When presenting valuations to buyers, you should create them in a report or on a spreadsheet using comparable sales. I discuss this in detail later in the book, but for the most part, you just compare financials from the sought-after company to comparable sales of similar companies to come up with a valuation range of prices for the business being sought. The report gives buyers confidence that their offer is fair, but it also displays to the buyers that they are dealing with a professional and competent agent who understands how analyze information and make judgments in a business-like manner.

When a buyer is ready to make the offer, you should put the offer in writing including all of the terms and conditions and have the buyer sign it. You can do this with a Letter of Intent (LOI) or an offer to purchase (Asset Purchase Agreement). It is a good idea to also get a check for the down payment, but this can be done after the seller agrees and signs a final purchase agreement as well. If there is a major contingency, then you may use a LOI and make the offer (i.e. the offer price is $520,000 based on an asset appraisal of $200,000 and the price is to be reduced dollar for dollar with a reduction in asset appraisal value). An offer with a LOI does not include a down payment. It is simply a letter saying that the buyer will pay a certain price if the seller can meet certain criteria. If so, then the buyer and seller would immediately sign a contract and a down payment is to be put in escrow at that time. An agent who can learn to skillfully use LOIs to move an interested buyer from just being interested to a contract, will be very successful as an agent.

CHAPTER 5

Procedure When Working with Buyers

Never confuse motion with action. —Benjamin Franklin

Accelerated Learning Tip

Buyers are attracted to listings like fish after lures. You may be working with a buyer one moment and the next thing you know, the buyer won't return your calls for many weeks. The truth is, they found another listing on the internet and started working with another broker. Nine times out of ten, they decide that they won't buy that other listing and prefer working with me as opposed to the other broker. This has happened hundreds of times to me. The reasons they come back are because I am honest, reliable, knowledgeable, and helpful to them. They see how some of the other brokers operate and decide that they trust me and can rely on me for advice and assistance.

Real-Life Experience

I get referrals from residential real estate agents all the time. They just don't understand the business brokerage industry and to try to run buyers around "looking" at businesses will exhaust anybody. One referral came to me from an agent who had a client looking for a pizza restaurant to buy anywhere between Jupiter and Miami. This poor agent was driving across Florida to show listings that were two and half hours from her house and two hours apart from each other. Anyway, I downloaded all the pizza restaurants in the business MLS that fit his budget, sent him a list of the towns they were located in and asked him to tell me which towns he would not like to live near. This narrowed the list down from 15 to 3. Since pizza restaurants are heavily reliant on location for customers, I asked him to choose the locations that he thinks will generate the most business. This narrowed it down to two within five miles of each other. We made an offer on one, but the offer was rejected, so we made an offer on the other and it was accepted, and we closed in less than a month.

The Elevator Pitch

To sum up working with buyers: Call all buyers immediately, set up an in-person meeting if possible, let them tell you what they want and why they want it, find out how much money they have to spend, find out their strong business traits, search businesses that appear to be good listings that fit their budget and their strong traits, call the listing agents, gather the listing information, value the listings, and have your buyers make offers. Do this as many times as you can each week and you can plan to sell one or two businesses each month.

Now, let's go through the procedure in detail.

Call Buyers Immediately After Receiving a Lead

It's imperative for new agents to learn to telephone buyers and not to use text or email for contacting clients, especially for the initial contact. It's unlikely that a text or email can generate the same rapport with buyers as a telephone call or a face-to-face meeting. Buyers may contact several agents when searching the internet for businesses and will chose the agent they feel most comfortable with. The only way to develop the necessary rapport is in person or over the phone. Remember that the industry average for agents is one in 13 closings for buyers who they met in person and one in 36 for buyers that they speak to on the telephone. Calling also demonstrates reliability, promptness, and respect; by showing these qualities, you will have a better chance at gaining a buyer's confidence. Also, psychological studies have demonstrated how buyers make up their minds very quickly during the sales process about if they are willing to buy something from a particular salesperson. On the telephone, it's done in a matter of seconds, and in person, it's a few minutes. Calling back immediately or answering you telephone should give you the edge that you need to win the buyer over, but especially try to get meetings with as many buyers as possible.

As previously mentioned, and well worth repeating, 90 percent of buyers who call will not buy the listing that they inquire about and 50 percent of those buyers will not buy a listing in the same category as the listing that they inquire about. Why would so many buyers inquire about listings they don't sincerely want to purchase? In order to answer this question, it is important to examine the psyche of the average buyer: Most buyers are first-time buyers and they are not sure of what business type will suit their needs. They have some money to invest and need to generate an income stream from that money, and they are looking to either replace a job or create supplemental income to their job. Their initial online search will reveal thousands of business listings, all with confusing numbers and sales pitches, therefore you will need to lead them through the search and clarify things for them.

Step-by-Step Guide

1. You should call every buyer immediately upon receiving a lead. If you are busy, you should still call immediately and schedule a time to call the buyer back.

2. Since the idea of a call is to develop a rapport with buyers, you must be friendly

and courteous at the outset.

3. Asking questions during the initial phone call will help give you a sense of the buyer's needs. Although it is important to ask questions about the buyer's business experience, skills, and finances, you should also tread lightly at this point because it is more important to develop a rapport than to qualify the buyers.

4. Agents who offer guidance to first time buyers will have the best chance of developing a rapport with them and having them continue as clients until they purchase something. Some topics of interest for agents to discuss are how much money buyers have; SBA loans and how buyers can leverage their money; their expected timing of a purchase, and categories of businesses that might suit the buyer's dominant business trait.

5. Agents should remember not to focus the conversation with buyers on particular businesses that they first inquire about but rather to focus on the buyer's needs and skills to get a list of criteria to better fit the buyer to other listings. Remember that 90percent of buyers will not buy the listing they called about and 50percent will not even buy in the same listing category. I can't repeat this enough. It is very important.

6. Whenever possible, meet with buyers, this increases your chances of closing deals with those buyers by more than double. At the very least, try to set up a 20-minute meeting at a local coffee shop
    *   Remember that a buyer's purpose of a call is to find out information about a particular business of interest and your purpose is to get a meeting with the buyer. The two purposes are not necessarily conflicting, but you'll need to be prepared to delay the buyer's purpose until after you've achieved your purpose. If you were to break down and give the buyer the business information, then you are not as likely to get your meeting and therefore have decreased your chances of a sale
    *   Start by explaining that not all businesses on the market are good businesses and not all are priced right. If the buyer is able to meet with you, you can promise to go over some examples of good and bad businesses. You can also explain that you have a procedure for buyers to follow in order to find the best businesses and buy them and that you would be happy to go over that procedure with the buyer at a meeting.

Qualifying Your Buyers

What the wise man does at the beginning, the fool does at the end. —Warren Buffet

The term prequalify can be confused with qualify by new agents. Prequalify means to get your buyers or your businesses prequalified by a bank for financing. Qualifying buyers, on the other hand, means interviewing buyers in order to determine whether or not they meet certain qualifications necessary and have the financial ability to purchase particular businesses. This is done verbally at first, and eventually, it should be reduced to writing in order to show sellers that these buyers meet the necessary qualifications to purchase the business.

Qualifying Buyers Financially

When qualifying buyers financially, the first step is for agents to simply ask buyers how much money they have available and where the money is coming from. It's common to have buyers who are borrowing money from friends or family to purchase a business. It would also be important to know whether they need a loan, because, this is a good time to start the loan pre-approval process. A loan letter can be a great bargaining tool for buyers because sellers know they will get paid in full at closing. If a buyer only has $100,000 and is inquiring about a $300,000 business, then you should ask how the buyer expects to raise the extra money needed to purchase the business. More likely than not, the buyer intends on asking the seller to lend the money. This may work on certain listings, but you will want to know this ahead of time, so you don't waste time looking at listings that can only be purchased with cash or bank financing.

The Small Business Association (SBA) is a government entity set up to back business acquisition loans made by banks. SBA loans are the major source of all small business acquisition loans from banks. Prequalifying your buyers entails getting them prequalified for a SBA business acquisition loan with a bank.

Qualifying Buyers for Experience

The next step is to determine what relevant experience and background a buyer has in order to determine which businesses would be most suitable. Again, this is done by simply asking the buyer relevant questions; but eventually, you should have the buyer fill out a profile form, which will detail this experience and provide some comfortability for the seller that this buyer is qualified to run the business desired, especially when seller-financing is involved. As a side note, most franchise businesses will have their own qualification forms and approval processes for buyers. Some franchises even have training classes that buyers must complete with a passing grade prior to purchasing the business.

Qualifying Buyers as International Investors

Finally, citizenship can play into whether a buyer is qualified or not. Many foreign nationals come to the United States seeking citizenship through the EB5 or legal status through the E2 visa program. If this is the case, you will need to work closely with an immigration attorney in order to qualify each business and each buyer for the visa program desired. Only certain businesses will qualify for each individual buyer, and agents will need the help of an attorney to make this determination. There is a section in this book that deals with the qualification process for investor visas.

Step-by-Step Guide

1. You should initially look to verbally qualify buyers financially, but eventually in writing with a financial form before the information needs to be shared with a seller or a listing agent.

2. If you determine that a buyer needs an acquisition loan, then have the buyer immediately speak to an SBA lender to get a pre-qualification done. SBA lenders are easy to find. Most major banks are SBA lenders and their salespersons will contact you once you join a business broker association. A pre-qualification entails having a buyer simply speak to a bank officer about the possibility of an acquisition loan. Most banks will not start the formal application process until a business is identified, but it is important that the buyer establish this initial relationship and receive an idea of the amount of loan money available to him. Many banks will issue buyers a letter stating that they have been pre-qualified for a certain amount of money. Also, your buyer may be disqualified which is equally important to know.

   • Alternatively, a loan broker can prequalify a buyer more formally by pulling a credit report. SBA lenders don't want to pull a buyer's credit report because they have a limited time after that to make the loan, therefore, with SBA lenders, the pre-qualification process is more informal. The other reason to consider using loan brokers is that they will keep on top of things and make sure that your buyers submit applications and documents as necessary. If they don't do the legwork and follow up, then you will have to do it. Brokers do charge borrowers a fee, but they provide an important service to them for that fee.

   • A SBA loan is a government backed loan which can be used for business acquisition for up to 90 percent of the purchase price. Often times, borrowers are given an operating capital loan in conjunction with the main SBA loan and the total financing can come to 100 percent of the purchase price. Borrowers still need to have 10 to 15 percent of the purchase price to buy the company, however, the SBA may still be willing to back a loan for 100 percent of the price.

   • A SBA loan can be a great tool to use with buyers: When buyers receive a preliminary approval, they may also receive a letter to show that they can purchase a business with bank financing. This gives the buyer leverage with sellers, as if they are paying cash. It makes sellers happy if they don't have to finance any of the purchase price. Alternatively, if buyers don't apply for pre-qualification but need financing, it indicates to sellers that they are not serious buyers or have poor credit.

3. You should qualify buyers for business experience and find their dominant business trait in order to properly suggest listings or categories of businesses that may be suitable for them. Eventually, you should have buyers fill out a buyer profile form. Serious and ready buyers should not have an issue giving you their background information. If they don't want to share this information, then this should indicate to you that those buyers are not ready and avoid wasting your time with them.

4. If buyers are foreign investors seeking visas, you should immediately introduce them to an immigration attorney prior to doing a business search. You should absolutely require that buyers hire an attorney and pay a retainer fee in order to continue searching for businesses with you. This is a necessary and important step in the business buying process for foreign investors. If they won't retain or consult with an attorney, then they are not ready to purchase a business. Without the advice and guidance of an immigration attorney, they will not know what business will qualify them for a visa. Also, you should maintain contact with their attorney and have them review businesses prior to entering into purchase agreements to make sure the businesses meet the visa criteria. The criteria for business visas is very subjective. Some businesses will qualify for some buyers and not others.

Searching for Businesses

To hell with circumstances: I create opportunities. —Bruce Lee

During their initial business search on the web, buyers generally pick business types that appear easy to operate, and then call each agent shown on the websites for those listings. Many buyers will choose gas stations, coin laundries, and retail shops, which appear easy enough to operate. Unfortunately, these businesses are not always easy to operate, and buyers need to be advised about the risks associated with these businesses.

Let's look at owning a gas station, for example. Gas stations are open 7 days a week, 24 hours a day, or nearly that. Gas station owners will need to be able to handle problems at all hours of the night and on weekends, as they receive problem calls from managers, landlords, suppliers, the police, the fire department, and more. There are many regulations and inspections associated with owning a gas station, which can result in hefty fines against an unaware owner. Gas stations have a very slim profit margin and the acquisition cost is high because the new owner will have to come up with a fuel deposit for the supplier which may be in the hundreds of thousands of dollars. If your buyers are okay with all of this, then gas stations might be a good fit for them. The point is, first time buyers need to be counseled about buying businesses that suit their business backgrounds and dominant business traits. You can't tell somebody not to buy a gas station, but you can ask if it's okay for you to search other types of businesses that may better fit their needs. Talk to your buyers about how you think they match up to owning a gas station verse owning different types of businesses. Discuss the benefits and drawbacks of both and how each suit their dominant business trait and experience.

As a new agent, you will need to develop a sense of which business types are suitable for which buyers and how to locate those businesses. This takes time, but networking will help shorten the learning curve. It's important to call agents who have listings in the categories that your buyers are inquiring about. This is done for two reasons: first, to get information about those companies from the listing agents; and secondly, to develop a network of agents who deal in those industries, which will help you put deals together with other future buyers. It's important to note that listing agents gain insight into similar listings for sale by virtue of working with buyers and sellers in that particular industry. It's not uncommon for agents to pick up other listings in the same industry just by having their ear to the ground while working the original listing. You can think of agents with listings as experts in that listing category.

The bottom line is, good agents will develop and use their knowledge and experience to guide and counsel buyers as they search for businesses. On the other hand, agents who fetch information for buyers on listings without regard to compatibility will fail because too many issues will remain barriers for those buyers. Developing good skills as a counselor and deal-maker will allow for a greater efficiency when working with buyers; hence, less time spent with buyers and more closed deals as a result. It's tempting to take the shortcut and just send buyers information without counseling them through the business buying process but taking the shortcut will not allow you to become a great agent with a great closing ratio.

After you have spoken with buyers and prequalified them, you need to search for businesses that match their criteria. Normally, a search should be started on the local business MLS website because MLS listings are definitely co-brokered and a lot of the information that you need to sell those listings is easily accessible. The next source of listings is BizBuySell.com and BizQuest.com, these are the second most comprehensive sources of listings. Loopnet.com is another possible source for businesses that contain real estate, like, gas stations, storage places, or hotels. There are other commercial sites that have business listings, but they don't have a large inventory and many times the listings are expired or sold, and the information isn't always current. You should constantly be on the lookout for similar secondary sites, especially regional sites in your local business area because more sites are popping up with the growth of the internet. Furthermore, for industry specific listings, you can do an internet search for listings in a certain area (i.e. gas stations for sale Miami). This type of search should turn up a few websites from local brokers who specialize in those types of listing. Contact those brokers and ask if they are willing to co-broker their listings. If so, you should get a cooperation agreement prior to introducing your buyers to those listings. If listings in a certain category are scarce but in demand by buyers, it's possible to have buyers pay your commission even if listing brokers refuse to share their fee. Gas stations have been difficult to find in the past few years and buyers have been willing to pay a fee to buyer-brokers who locate high volume stations for sale.

Finally, don't be afraid to knock on doors or call business owners and ask if they are willing to sell if you have a buyer that they can meet right away. It's fairly easy to locate business owners of each category, you simply go online to Manta. com or YP.com and search businesses of that type in the area you need.

Step by Step Guide

1. Check the local business MLS first for the listing category of business being inquired about.

2. Also check for other similar businesses which may interest your buyers. For example, if they are interested in a dry cleaner, then you can also look for commercial laundries.

3. It's a good idea to search for two or three businesses that match the category of the listing that the buyers inquire about and three businesses outside of that category. Remember that you only have a 50percent chance of each buyer buying a listing in the category inquired about.

   - It's important to try to be as helpful and relevant a source of information for buyers as possible. Do not simply fetch information on listings that buyers are inquiring about and move on to the next listing or next buyer. Remember to take your time to counsel buyer through the process in order to earn their loyalty and focus their attention on the most relevant businesses.

   - Buyers are looking for an income stream or an investment; statistics show that 90percent will not buy the listing they inquire about and 50percent will eventually buy something outside of the industry that they inquire about. You need to remember this and play by those rules.

4. If you have trouble locating a match for your buyer, call some agents in your

local business MLS who have the same type of business listings that the buyers are seeking. Those agents will have more knowledge about similar businesses for sale than any other agents.

5. Similarly, when you are looking for a specific type of business which may be in short supply, some listing agents will specialize in business types; for example, some agents may only sell gas stations. Those agents keep their ear to the ground in that industry and may likely know of other possible leads. It's important for you to develop a network of agents who specialize in different types of businesses and keep their contact information in a directory.

6. You can continue searching for similar businesses matching buyers' criteria on Bizbuysell.com, Bizquest.com, and possibly Loopnet.com.

   - If a match is found, you can make an inquiry with the listing agent to check whether they will co-broker the listing and how much the commission split is.

   - Some brokers are part of a network of cooperating brokers on these websites, but some brokers do not participate and will not co-broker their listings.

   - You should always get a cooperation agreement with the listing brokerage prior to introducing buyers to any listings from agents who are not part of a cooperating network. So, until you get a cooperation agreement with that brokerage, you cannot show that listing to your client and expect to be paid a commission.

   - When a broker chooses not to cooperate with other agents, they still have the choice to cooperate whenever they want. Therefore, if you approach them with a legitimate buyer and they don't have a good buyer of their own, they may accept your offer to cooperate and share a commission. But remember that these agents are not used to sharing and they can be like the bratty kids in grade school. They can offer you any amount of commission they want, and it isn't always a 50 percent split. There are no hard and fast rules here, everything is a matter of negotiation. If you are not able to negotiate a satisfactory commission split, then you don't have to show the listing to your buyer.

   - Of course, your buyer is free to go to that broker independently of you, but you wouldn't receive a commission at that point unless your buyer signed an agreement with you to work exclusively with you. That's called a Buyer Broker agreement and the buyer would be responsible for paying you a commission, not the seller or seller's agent.

7. If all else fails, try using an internet search to match your buyer's criteria. Some

brokers maintain their own private websites and do not advertise on the mainstream sites. Some of these brokers will cooperate and share their commission. If not, it's possible to have your buyers pay your fee and to let the listing agent earn his commission from the seller. To do this, you'd have your buyer sign an agreement to pay you a commission of a certain amount. Some brokers will use a one-time showing agreement, but I've always accepted my buyers verbal promise. It will be up to your broker to decide how you handle this.

8. Last, but not least, you should search Manta.com, Hoovers.com, or YP.com business directories and retrieve lists of existing businesses that match the criteria. Contact the owners and ask if they would be interested in selling if you bring them your buyer. Most new agents are surprised at the great response they get. This is a great way to pick up new listings. It really works.

Buyers Must Sign a Non-Disclosure Agreement (NDA)

Discipline is just doing the same thing the right way whether anyone's watching or not.
—Michael J. Fox

It's imperative that you have each buyer sign a Non-Disclosure Agreement (also, referred to as a Disclosure, a Confidentiality Agreement, or a Non-Circumvent Non-Disclosure) for each listing prior to giving buyers any identifying details about a business. Furthermore, each listing must have a separate signed NDA from each buyer. The NDA protects agents from liability due to the exposure of confidential information about a seller's business. It also protects sellers from willful or negligent acts of buyers that could have devastating effects on a seller's business. The NDA helps protect sellers, agents, and brokers in the event of a lawsuit; therefore, agents should never forgo a signed NDA prior to divulging any detailed information about a listing. All listing information is confidential to the listing agents and their associates (members of the MLS, accountants, attorneys, or loan brokers associated with the deal) and should not be shared with buyers prior to receiving signed NDAs.

Occasionally, you may run into some pushy buyers who ask for the names or addresses of businesses, so they can drive by and see if they like the location before signing a NDA. Don't do it. This is not acceptable, and you should not give buyers any identifying information. Think of it this way, the fact that they want the business address to see by themselves means that they already do not want to work with you. At any rate, it's legally imperative that you obtain a signed NDA prior to disclosing any confidential information about sellers' businesses, especially names or addresses. The exception to this rule is to speak about information that is already available to buyers in advertisements or on website teasers. For example, you may say, "We have a nice medium-size grocery store in the area with sales above $1.5 Million." This is done without giving away the seller's name, address, or financial details. Follow up with, "I'd be happy to show you more information about this business, but I'll need you to sign a NDA first."

Occasionally, buyers will object to signing NDA paperwork for no good reason. They are simply scared to sign anything. These buyers are generally unacquainted with the business sales process and are afraid of signing a legal document that is unfamiliar to them. Perhaps they are associating buying a business with buying a home. With residential real estate, they may be told by their attorney not to sign anything before the attorney reviews it. The best course of action is for you to explain that, unlike real estate, business buyers are given access to confidential information about a seller's business and an unscrupulous buyer could possibly ruin the business. If buyers still won't sign after they are explained how sellers are entitled to protection, then they can hire an attorney and have the attorney review the NDA. Don't waste too much time trying to convince them to sign it. When a relationship starts out on the wrong foot, it usually only gets worse. You are better off spending your time with buyers who are ready to listen to your advice.

Step-by-Step Guide

1. Don't release any identifying or confidential information about a business listing until you have a signed NDA from any buyer.

2. Every listing should have a signed NDA from each buyer.

3. To create a NDA, you will need to obtain your buyer's complete identifying information, including, name, address, telephone and email. A busy agent will be sending hundreds of disclosures each year and the process needs to become simple and routine.

   - The easiest way to do this is to create a pdf document and send it via an E-Sign program. Electronic signature is legal in Florida and you should check to see if it's a legally binding form of signature in your state.

   - Many MLS associations and commercial websites have a method for distributing NDAs to buyers; whereby, buyers can click to print out a NDA for the listing they are looking at, sign it, scan it and email or fax it back to you.

Send Buyers Information

After your buyers sign a NDA, you can provide detailed information about a prospective business. You can do this in-person, via email, or fax. The first thing buyers should see is the listing information sheet. This is a one-page summary of the business information along with a summary of the financials. Most business

MLS associations allow agents to print out this sheet or email it to clients once a NDA is signed.

The most common error made by new agents is failing to follow up to review the information after emailing it to their buyers. Remember that buyers need counseling and guidance. A listing sheet looks like a compilation of numbers and abbreviations. Even when buyers are able to disseminate the information, the fact that their agent fails to follow up, gives them the impression of apathy or that the you are too busy to take the time to assist with their search. Good agents will call buyers and review the information in person or on the telephone. This is not only professional, but it will help you get immediate feedback on whether the listing or category of listings will work for that buyer. Doing this reassures buyers that you are making efficient use of your time and contributes towards developing the necessary rapport to obtain buyer loyalty.

If I had a nickel for every time an agent told me they sent an NDA but haven't hear back from their buyer, I would be wealthy. It's simply counterintuitive to let a listing try to sell itself. Although the job is not a high-pressure sales job, you do have to do some selling. Just remember that you need to be a problem solver and a dealmaker. If you aren't communicating with your client, then you aren't solving problems and won't make any deals. Follow up calls are simple; the buyer should actually be expecting to hear from you. It may go something like this, "Hi, Mary, this is Bill from Florida Business Brokers. I received your email inquiry about the X-business and sent you a NDA to sign. Once you sign that, I'll be able to send you more information and discuss some details about the business with you." If you are leaving a voicemail, then say, "Hi, Mary, this is Bill from Florida Business Brokers, please call me back if you'd like to discuss the business that you inquired about." The difference with leaving a voicemail, is that you want to speak to the buyer. Remember that your chances of selling a business to buyers goes up as your communication with buyers becomes more personal. Ideally, you want to take the relationship with buyers from email, to telephone, to in-person meetings in order to attain your best results and an overall high percentage of sales.

1. After receiving a signed NDA from your buyers, you should email them a listing information sheet. This is a general outline of the opportunity and the first source of information that buyers should receive.

2. Call or meet with buyers immediately after sending them the information. Do not wait more than a day to follow up about the listing information that you send, or your buyers may look for other listings and find other agents to work with.

Email and Call the Listing Agent

To make a difference in the real world is to put ten times as much into everything as anyone thinks is reasonable. —Daniel Vasella

Many buyers will come to you for information on listings that are part of a business MLS and therefore they were listed by other agents, referred to as listing agents. The requirement to call listing agents is another step in the process that is often overlooked by new agents to their detriment. In fact, this is where business gets done: It's absolutely critical not to skip this step for a number of reasons. For starters, this is how new agents develop a network. Their network becomes a tool to use to get more deals done than other agents who never develop a good network. Secondly, the most accurate and complete information on businesses cannot be obtained without calling the listing agents. The listing agents may or may not respond to your emails. As rude as that sounds, it's a fact in the business world that emails may either fail to obtain a response or they receive a delayed response. Time is money and you don't want to lose your buyers. Furthermore, even if you do get a response, listing agents may answer with a simple attachment or a quick explanation of how to go about showing their listings. By calling, instead, it allows a question and answer session which should generate detailed information about the businesses sought. Accordingly, phone calls to listings agents should provide enough information to either rule out these listings immediately or indicate that these listings are good ones to pursue. By and large, listing agents will be honest and explanatory on the telephone; whereas, in emails, they will be short and indirect, that is, if you get a response at all.

Here is an example of how a telephone call to an agent may go. And remember, if buyers like you, they will want to deal with you, it's human nature and something that you should take advantage of to help boost your sales. Simply, start out by introducing yourself as a business broker agent with a good buyer who is interested in the agent's listing.

"Hi, John Doe listing agent, this is Bill, a business broker with Florida Business Brokers. I'm calling about your listing X-business and have a potentially good fit for a buyer. My buyer has [this much money] and [this much experience, etc.]. Do you have more information that you can share with me? Is it still available?"

Don't be afraid to interject some small talk if the listing agent is available to have a discussion. You are colleagues working in the same industry and it's expected that you would ask how business is going or discuss other business-related information. The other reason to do this is that next time you call this agent, he or she will remember you and the conversation will flow even easier. This will help you get the information that you are calling about. Some agents are friendlier than others and you'll get to know who will share information with you and who won't, but if you only text or email, you'll never get to know the other agents in this way.

Another reason to call listing agents is that they are the best source of a sales pitch for the business being sold: think of listing agents as the "listing cheerleader." The spiel that the agents deliver to you can be used and repeated to your buyers as your sales pitches. Telephoning listing agents on every listing will pay off by saving valuable time and by providing the information that you need to sell each business sought.

Step-by-Step Guide

1. Upon receiving a signed NDA, you should immediately call the listing agent for each business being pursued. There is always more information than what is shown on the listing sheet. Remember that time is money and your buyers are waiting for this information. The sooner you get it, the better chance you have at keeping your buyers interested and making deals.

2. After your initial phone call to the listing agents, follow up with emails to the listing agents with a copy of the signed NDAs, and request any further written information about the listings.

   - Emailing the listing agents will remind them to send copies of the listing memoranda. A listing memorandum is a comprehensive description of the business and the financials. Many agents work from a cellphone and will not be able to send the memorandum until they reach a computer. The email then serves as a reminder.

   - Occasionally, you will run into an unscrupulous listing agent who will not respond to emails or telephone calls. Follow up. This can be annoying; however, some agents don't understand the benefits of co-brokering listings. Their lack of response indicate that they have a buyer of their own. Remember, most buyers that seek a particular listing will not buy it, therefore, these unscrupulous agents will need to seek your buyer after their buyer is gone and you can expect to get in touch with them in a few days.

Buyers go Bye-Bye Without Your Attention

Pray as if everything depends on God. Work as if everything depends on you. —John Wesley

It's a good idea to use a calendar program to schedule follow up calls with buyers. You may typically handle five or more buyers at any time and tracking their contact information, storing client data, and scheduling meetings and calls can be hectic without an orderly method and good software. A scheduling program with reminders will not only remind you to make calls, but it will also provide you the status of each buyer and remind you where you left off. Microsoft Outlook works well for this, as does most calendar programs on smartphones and tablets.

Some agents will look at 20 or more listings with a single buyer and never get an offer. This happens when agents get signed NDAs and send listing sheets to buyers without following up about each listing. I've mentioned this previously, but it is important and worth repeating: Agents who just get signed NDAs and then send listing sheets without following up are wasting their time and their buyer's time. Buyers can't get the complete picture of each business by simply looking at listing sheets. A good agent will schedule a follow up call within 24 hours to discuss each listing with every buyer. This follow up call gives buyers confidence that you are prepared, it also adds urgency and seriousness to the situation, which the buyer should notice from your follow up. This helps keep your clients in the right state of mind for moving forward towards purchasing a business and not just looking at listings.

Consequently, agents who take the time to give each listing a good review with their buyers and promote interest in each listing when possible, have a much greater success rate. This is especially true when a listing can be compared favorably to other listings that a buyer has been looking at. Buyers will pick up on your excitement and feel a sense of urgency that they need to pursue those particular listings.

One of the unfortunate things about working with buyers is that they come and go. Buyers may be in the middle of looking at businesses and be gone in an instant when they see other listings on the internet. This is not unusual, and you may lose contact with some buyers for a while. Most of these buyers will eventually return and ask to continue evaluating a previously reviewed business. Don't get discouraged when this happens. The internet has an abundance of business listings and buyers continually search and chase listings like fish after lures. In order to lessen this occurrence, aspire to be as helpful and informative as possible. You should try to stand out by being courteous, helpful, and responsive so that buyers will notice a difference between you and any other agents. Buyers should get the impression that you are responsive and courteous, and you are prepared to get the job done for them. If you remain professional during these times buyers should return your professionalism with future loyalty.

Step-by-Step Guide

1. You should use a calendar program to schedule follow up calls and meetings with buyers.

2. Always call buyers to discuss listing sheets after they are sent out. Agents should not wait longer than one day to follow up, as buyers may find other listings.

3. It is important to discuss the better listings in detail, to create a sense of ex-

citement and urgency.

4. You should always stay in contact with buyers and be responsive or buyers may find other listings from other agents and decide to work with them.

5. Buyers may find other listings even if you are courteous and helpful. You should be patient and be ready to work with the buyers when they return, most should return.

Advise Buyers to Make Offers

Intelligence is the ability to adapt to change. —Stephen Hawking

Some agents will argue that this subject is incorrectly placed ahead of the next subject in this book: Arrange a Meeting or Showing. Here lies the difference between successful and unsuccessful business agents.

Since most business Asset Purchase Agreements are non-binding on buyers, or can be drawn up to read that way, buyers have some time to withdraw or cancel their offer before their money is at risk. The due diligence clause specifically gives buyers a certain amount of time to review the financials and other documents and decide if they want to go through with the deal or cancel the deal and get their down payment back. This is the way a typical asset purchase agreement works, but you will have to read each different version that you use to make deals with, or have an attorney explain the due diligence clause in each to you. This is not to say that buyers should indiscriminately go around making offers on all businesses, that would be a waste of time, but in many cases where a buyer is interested in a business, an offer can be made in writing prior to any further review or meeting with the owner.

Having your buyers make offers prior to setting up meetings has some important benefits. First, it allows you to establish an agreed upon purchase price. Why have a meeting if a buyer is unable or unwilling to meet a seller's accepted price? You can waste a week or more on meetings and back and forth negotiations, just to find out that the buyer and seller can't agree on the salient issue: price. Secondly, and you should tell your buyers this, written offers get the seller's attention. Meetings bore sellers, but contracts excite them. If you have an excited seller, your buyer will have the upper hand in the meeting that follows. This gives your buyer leverage, whereas, normally sellers have most of the leverage and tend to wield it unnecessarily, as they are protectionists by nature: they are generally skeptical of buyers and not willing to release too much information initially. A written offer is the simplest way to unlock their protectionist nature.

Buyers are always on the lookout for risky transactions and they will hesitate to make offers due to a heightened perception of risk. Buyers contemplate losing everything in a transaction and are hesitant to take that next step. Remind buyers of their reasons for wanting to invest in a business and the potential of their investment. Let them know that they can back out of the deal within a time frame under the due diligence clause in the agreement if necessary. Also, advise them if they continue to look and not buy, some very good opportunities will pass them by. Give them encouragement and counseling: Compare and contrast different opportunities which they have sought in terms of risk and reward. Let them understand that some investments are better than others and some are riskier than others. Help them see the better investment when it comes along so they don't let it pass them by.

If a business opportunity has some risks associated with it, then you can help mitigate the risks for your buyer by advising the buyer to do one or more of the following: Lowering the offering price, asking for seller financing, structuring the deal with an earn out arrangement or an escrow holdback. These arrangements help shift some of the risk back to the seller. You should become adept at counseling clients on the risks and rewards of each opportunity to help generate offers. Think outside the box and create deals with the use of terms and conditions. For example, you can condition the sale on a certain valuation of the assets, with a stipulation for reducing the sales price based on a lower asset valuation; or, you may condition the sale on the seller signing a one-year management contract to operate the business which reduces the buyer's risk of losing customers due to a management change. There are many ways to make deals work if you have willing sellers and interested buyers. Good agents will be assertive and find ways to generate offers, in contrast, lesser agents will allow buyers to walk away from deals where they perceive risk without generating offers. It's not so much that buyers need convincing that their risks are not what they seem, it's more that buyers need to discuss the risks involved and talk through a strategy to either lower the price or to find another way to curtail the risks perceived. Sellers are not always willing to go along with a buyer's mitigation tactics but when they feel that the buyer involved is a good fit for their business, they are generally open to discussions about how to make the deal work. They may push back on an offer to lower the price but be open to an escrow holdback based on certain criteria. Businesses by their nature are high risk investments, so sellers should understand that they have to help alleviate buyers' concerns in order to make deals work. Agents who aren't able to convey this to buyers and sellers will not sell as many deals as agents who are able.

Your average buyers don't realize there are many different ways to structure deals and, in many cases, they can leverage their money. Some buyers are surprised when I tell them that they can get financing for a business acquisition. There are SBA loans, seller financing, equipment financing, hard money loans, lease to buy options, stock offerings, bonds, even a seller earn-out can be used. These are only some of the ways to put deals together, there are other ways to bring deals to the table, such as partnerships, equity investors, or leveraged buyouts. You will need to be creative and develop your deal making skills by thinking outside of the box. This will all come together for you with experience. In the beginning, you will focus on the most common types of deals that incorporate SBA loans and seller financing. You can graduate to more complicated deal structures as you gain experience.

Step-by-Step Guide

1. Most businesses sell for 25-35 percent less than their asking price. Discuss this with buyers and counsel them so that they are not turned off by the seemingly large amount of overpriced businesses.

2. Don't be afraid to approach sellers with low offers. You need to generate offers in order to sell businesses.

3. I use a financial analysis spreadsheet form to show buyers their Return on Investment (ROI) based on their offer. This keeps their reward in mind rather than allowing them to focus on the risks involved.

4. As long as your buyers are not locked into a deal under the due diligence clause, negotiate the deal and get a contract prior to setting up a showing or a meeting if possible.

5. Be creative and encourage buyers to talk about what they need in order to get them to buy a particular business. Handle the perception of risk involved by solving buyers' issues with creative thinking.

   • An offer may include seller financing even if there is no seller financing advertised.

   • An offer may include payouts over a few years based on future performance of the business.

6. Show buyers comparable sales reports for the industry to help them make their own valuation of a business.

7. Turn to more experienced agents if you need help. Your broker may be able to help if you are close but can't quite close a deal.

Arrange a Meeting or a Showing

You harvest what you plant, whether good or bad. —Proverbs 14:14

If a buyer shows interest in a listing, continue to promote interest by suggesting some questions that the buyer might ask the seller. If at all possible, get the buyer to make an offer and submit it in writing prior to arranging a meeting. Explain to your buyers how the due diligence clause works and that doing it this way gives buyers leverage with sellers and gets the price issue out of the way. Without an agreement on price, the deal has no chance of moving forward.

Written offers notwithstanding, if your buyers have questions, they usually need to be answered by the sellers or their agents. You can do this by setting up telephone conference calls or scheduling in-person meetings. Sometimes, meetings can be arranged at the businesses and sometimes they have to be done off premises so as not to alert the employees or customers of a potential sale.

Keep meetings short and on-point. It's okay to allow the initial pleasantries to go on for a while in the beginning because buyers and sellers have to be able to get along with each other in order to allow the deal to complete. If they don't get along, then you will not be able to make the sale. It's that simple. Sellers would rather close their business down than to sell to somebody they don't get along with. Allow buyers to introduce themselves to the sellers to start the meeting. Remember that the buyers know a lot more about sellers because they have been studying their businesses. Next, allow sellers to verbally say why they are selling. Nine times out of ten, this will be the buyers first question anyway. It's the salient issue and one that can't be avoided or covered up.

Supposing that your buyers and sellers do get along, direct the meetings by introducing topics or questions that you have previously discussed with your buyers. If somebody strays off point, then bring the conversation back on point. Limit the meeting to a previously agreed time limit and make sure to stick to that time. Occasionally, meetings will linger on as some people will tend to talk too much. Try not to be rude to these people but remember that they are taking up your time and keeping you from doing your job efficiently. Do your best to keep matters on-point and to keep the meeting limited to the scheduled time limit.

Since the buyer has already had a chance to read about the seller and the business, I usually start out by asking the buyer to introduce himself to the seller and give a little information about his background and why he is interested in this particular business. This normally generates some small talk between the buyer and seller and I'll often have to raise another question in order to get the meeting back on track. At this time, I'll go back to the seller and ask for a recap of the history of the business leading up to today and the reason he is selling. So, once this is complete, we've talked about the buyer's background and why the buyer wants to buy; and the seller's background and why the seller wants to sell. This is information that you must bring out in the discussion: knowing this information is the key to getting deals done. Just keep telling yourself that you need to ask questions to get the seller and the buyer to talk about what they each need. Knowing what they need will allow you to structure something that works for both of them. Of course, it goes without saying that if one of the parties is not discussing things openly or is being rude or not acting businesslike, then you should probably end the meeting because one or both parties are not interested in a deal. Just say thank you for your time, we'll be in touch and end the meeting. If it gets to this point, then everybody will be happy you spoke up and ended things early.

After meetings, you should be discussing the offer price with your buyers. Remember that you are spending a lot of time with these buyers and you have come this far. Now is the time to get offers. If your buyers don't want the business, that's fine and that becomes clear after some meetings; however, if they are still interested, don't let them ask for more information without putting the offer on the table. As difficult as it is, this is the time to be assertive with buyers and not to them make monotonous requests for more information. Remember, the due diligence clause gives them a way out, so they should be ready to sign an offer at this point.

The average agent sells one business for every 2.5 showings. Therefore, you should strive to bring as many buyers to this stage of the process as possible. At the same time, in order to increase your percentage to better than average, you will need to be assertive at this stage. If buyers are serious enough to go to showings, then ask for offers and remind buyers of the due diligence clause that allows them to back out under most circumstances. You can suggest an offer price based on how well the showing goes but do your best to solicit offers at the end of showings. If buyers are not willing to make offers immediately after showings, then it is unlikely that they will be making offers at all. If buyers have time to think about it, they will remember the bad aspects of the businesses and forget the good aspects and therefore will not commit.

Nine times out of ten, when my showings go well, buyers look like a deer in the headlights. They are trying to take everything in and analyze it. They have a good feeling about the meeting but are worried about taking the next step. Buyers are fearful because most of them have never been in this exact situation before. They know that they want to purchase a business, but finding the right business is something they are just not sure about how to do. They may feel good about the business and the showing, but they are unsure what that next step is. If they say anything, it's usually, "What do you think it's worth?" It's important to be prepared for this after showings and to be ready to guide your buyers on how to make formal offers. Whether they ask you what it's worth or not, just tell them you see that the showing went well and will assist them in making a formal offer as the next step. Tell them you'll go back to your office and put a written offer together for them to review and you'll call them later. You can suggest an offer price that is five or ten percent below what you would consider a fair purchase price to allow for negotiating. Remember to be assertive but not aggressive. Guidance is the key here: teach and guide your buyers to lead them through the purchase process.

Step-by-Step Guide

1. Showings are the most important step when selling businesses. It happens just

after or just prior to buyers making offers; therefore, agents should always strive to bring buyers to this stage of the sales process.

2. You should contact sellers' agents for meetings or showings; but, only after trying to get buyers to make offers.

3. It's not unusual for sellers or buyers to ask for conference calls prior to in-person meetings or showings: Sellers and buyers are concerned about wasting their time with unqualified buyers or incompatible businesses.

4. Conference calls can be set up through online services or by just using a cell-phone with additional calling capability.

5. Keep the meeting limited to the prearranged time limit and the prearranged topics. Don't be rude but run the meeting in a business-like manner.

6. Statistically, you should get an offer for every 2.5 buyers you arrange showings for; therefore, it's important to bring as many buyers to this stage in the buying process in order to close more deals. Remember that 2.5 is the statistical average. You want to strive for a better percentage.

7. Be assertive just after the showing when trying to solicit offers. If buyers don't make offers immediately following a showing, it is unlikely that they will make one at all.

How to Value a Business for a Buyer

Share prices fluctuate more than share values. —Sir John Templeton

There are different ways to value businesses; the most common are asset sales, and valuations based on percentage of gross sales or based on a multiple of net profits. The first scenario, is if the assets are worth more than the complete business, this is called an asset sale. In this case, the assets are valued using market value. There are industry experts who can help determine the fair market value of assets; in some industries, there are industry resale guides that you can use; or a business valuation expert can be hired. Valuation experts will charge for their services, so the parties involved will have to determine who bares the cost. Occasionally, you may see asset sales where the assets sell for more than their fair market value due to the location or the lease value. In other words, if the assets are in a desirable area or in a location with a low lease, it may add extrinsic value. Laundromats or gas stations are the most typical examples of this. If an existing gas station goes out of business because of poor management or a temporary real estate condition, then the value of the assets could well be worth more than the market value. As an example, if a gas station has a convenience store attached to it that doesn't sell beer and cigarettes due to some reason (whether due to religious reasons or a licensing issue) the gross sales will be low and the value of the gas station based on a percentage of earnings will be low. But if you value that same gas station as an asset sale, whether it is still operating or is out of business, the asset value to the purchaser will take into consideration that the new owner will sell beer and cigarettes and increase the sales revenue by hundreds of thousands of dollars. So, number-wise, you may be looking at a gas station that is valued at $50,000 based on earnings, or $200,000 based on asset values.

If a business is not an asset sale, then a variety of valuation methods may be used. However, the industry standard for small businesses is to use either a percentage of gross sales or a multiple of net profit. Generally, both of these methods will produce similar valuations. These methods are employed by evaluating comparable sales and looking at the ratios that similar companies have sold for. These ratios are reapplied to the company being valued to come up with a target sales price. The target sales price is then adjusted for market trend and the strength of the company to be sold. The adjustment variables are subjective, and a valuation price should be viewed as a range rather than an exact number. After the valuation is complete, the business can then be listed within the range or slightly above the target range depending on what your sellers wants. Generally, the higher the listing price, the longer the business will take to sell. Caution should be taken not to list businesses too high above the range to avoid the listings becoming stale. Stale is a real estate term that means once buyers have dismissed a listing due to the high price, they tend not to re-evaluate the listing even after the asking price is lowered. This sounds like psychological mumbo jumbo, but it really does happen.

Be careful with assets and inventory when looking at comparable sales information. Some business MLS will give you comparable sales with inventory and assets included in the sales prices, and some without. The point is that you must compare apples to apples. If your comparable sales include inventory and assets in the sales prices, then you must look at the business to be valued with inventory and assets included. You should also note that some unscrupulous brokers will include try to sell businesses by setting a business price and asking extra for the inventory. This is not standard and may not be ethical if sold to an unsuspecting first-time buyer. I will discuss this later in this book.

There are other variables that come into play when pricing a business; such as, earnings growth, future expected earnings, sales contracts, accounts receivable, intangible assets, location, lease value, market trend, and industry trend. Unfortunately, many of these items don't have a definite market value, you will have to discuss these things with your clients, accountants, attorneys, other agents, lenders, or any other people in your network who may be able to give advice on the subject. I find that sellers are usually the best source of information in this situation. They know their industry and how their business compares to competitors. A more established and more competitive company will command a higher than average price, as compared to a new or poorly competitive company. I'm not saying that your buyers have to rely on sellers to price the business for them, I'm just saying that their insight in the industry is a good source of information and most sellers are happy to share their knowledge in a frank manner. It doesn't hurt to ask, and you can take the thoughts for what you may, based on your impression of their interpretation.

Step-by-Step Guide

Procedure for valuing businesses using a multiple of cash flow or a percentage of gross sales

1. Search for comparable businesses sales (comps). You can find them through a business MLS or a commercial service. Also, the Business Reference Guide by Tom West or BIZCOMPS online at www.bvresources.com are great sources of information on comparable business sales.

2. Check if the comparable sales include assets and inventory in their ratios. If not, then you will have to add them back to your comparable sales and recalculate the ratios.

3. Adjust the comps for locations and size of businesses to fit your listing by removing any comps that don't fit. Location is normally not too important but try to stay in the same state. If there are not enough comparable sales in the same state, then you may look nationally.

4. Obtain the average multipliers for gross sales and net income (Sold Price/ Sales) and (Sold Price/Net Income).

5. Now, take the gross sales and the net income numbers from the business being sold (you should try to use an average of the last three years, if not, use what you have) and multiply those numbers by the respective average ratios shown on your comp report.

   • Example: Average Gross Sales past 3 years times the industry average multiple: $500,000 x 30percent = $150,000 (valuation based on Gross Sales multiple)

   • Example: Average Net Income past 3 years times the industry average ratio:

   • $140,000 x 1.3 = $182,000 (value based on Net Income ratio)

6. This will give you two different, but similar valuation numbers. These numbers indicate the approximate selling price that your seller can expect based on averages. These numbers together represent a value range.

   • Example: Value range = $150,000 to $182,000

7. If a business owns real estate, then the real estate may be sold separately or

with the business. If it is being sold with the business, then add the value of the real estate to the business valuation range. Real estate values are obtained through similar comparable sales figures that can be obtained from your local commercial MLS or from a commercial service that keeps track of comparable sales figures.

8. Occasionally, there is excess value that needs to be added, like, spare equipment that is not used to conduct business at the current time, or excess inventory. You can add anything of extra value to the price of the business.

9. The final value range should be adjusted up or down based on other variables such as the strength of the business in question and the market trend. This is a little bit of science and a little bit of art. As you gain experience, your value ranges will tighten up and become more accurate.

   - Example: Value range = $150,000 to $182,000 plus 10percent due to above average industry strength = $165,000 to $200,000 (adjusted valuation range).

Submitting Offers

If you rest you rust. —Helen Hayes

When your buyers are ready to make offers, get the offers in writing before calling the listing agents. This shows that you are serious and professional, which is the same attitude that you want replicated by the sellers' agents, even if the offers are eventually rejected. Sellers' agents deal with many buyer's agents and many offers for each listing. Many agents do not act professional to the exasperation of the listing agents. To earn the respect of the sellers' agents, don't waste their time or yours with buyers who are not ready to formally commit to the purchase. Know your buyers and their needs, relay this information efficiently to the sellers' agents and always submit offers in writing. Acting this way will help earn you respect and get your buyers the attention they deserve on each listing. You need to stand out from the crowd of unprofessional agents by emanating professionalism right from the initial contact with seller's agents.

Some listings are more desirable than others and therefore will draw more attention from buyers. Generally, these are low priced and high-volume retail businesses like coin laundries and gas stations. These listings will likely get multiple offers in a short period of time. When you get buyers interested in this type of listing, call the listing agents immediately and discuss the terms of possible offers. Whether the feedback is good, bad, or even unreasonable, it's important to make the call to prevent from losing the deals to competing buyers. You can start by saying that you have a serious buyer that you already prequalified for the listing (make sure you do a prequalification before calling) then say that you understand that the listing must have offers already or that it soon will, and you would like to see if you can bring your buyer to a showing. Make it clear that your buyer is prequalified and ready to make an offer. This is information that will get passed by in a text or email, but on the telephone, you can make this perfectly clear to the agent. An open line of communication is very important to avoid losing out on a deal; and I mean talking, not texting and emailing. Texts and emails are sometimes misinterpreted or passed up and forgotten. Listing agents and sellers are generally in a better bargaining position than buyers due to a lack of similar businesses for sale at any one time, and their feedback should not be taken lightly. If a listing agent thinks that a buyer is not serious or not ready to commit, that buyer will become a lesser priority than other buyers, especially to those who go through the listing agent directly. If listing agents brings their own buyers to the table, then they get the entire commission, therefore, listing agents always want their buyers to enter contracts on their deals. Stay in contact with listing agents and use an open line of communication to keep your buyers in front of their sellers. Don't be afraid to ask about any other offers or buyers. They may not give you specifics, but they will usually give you general hints. Keep pushing and be assertive with these deals as long as you have serious buyers.

Make the case to listing agents for the price and terms of your offers. This is where deals get done: if listing agents are not happy with offers, they may not present them well to their sellers and the chances of making deals are slim. When listing agents are not impressed with offers, it makes the offer presentation to their sellers difficult or even embarrassing; hence their presentation will be weak, and you have a slim chance for a deal. Consider revising offers that are not received well prior to having them presented to sellers. Put the offers on hold and discuss possible changes with your buyers. If your buyers are able to make changes, this will increase your chances of making more deals. Listing agents are more likely to convince their sellers to accept or re-negotiate a reasonable offer rather than a lowball offer. That's not to say that you can't or shouldn't make lowball offers, just that you must be aware of the burden that you will have to overcome when making offers that do not impress listing agents.

Occasionally, listings agent won't respond to your calls and messages despite the fact that you have a signed offer to present. Usually it means the listing agents are working with buyers of their own and are in the process of getting offers. This is not ethical and against the rules of most business listing associations; however, it is a reality that you will have to deal with. Continue to follow up and try to make contact with the agents, but don't be harassing or annoying. Remember, business brokers are a small group and it is common to see the same agents time and again. Making business acquaintances and adding agents to your network will be much more valuable over time than creating enemies. Persistence and patience should pay off over time. Of course, you can report blatant abuses of real estate regulations or MLS rules, but generally it's a game of "he said, she said" and few and far between wind up with any sanction or settlement. At the same time, if you put in your formal complaint with your MLS, you can hope that other agents do the same. After enough complaints, the agent may get thrown out of the MLS.

Offers can either be made with a LOI or a purchase agreement. LOIs may be used to submit offers with loose ends; in other words, if an offer contained an important stipulation or if it was made contingent on a fact or document that was yet to be proved, then a LOI is likely warranted. LOI are normally non-binding because they are presented without consideration (down payment). You can think of them of as an agreement to agree: If a LOI is accepted by a seller, then the two parties will negotiate and sign a legally binding contract (purchase agreement) after the stipulation contained in the LOI is met by the seller. Although LOI are non-binding, they are a tool to be used to assist with negotiating major issues. When negotiating issues, you can avoid miscommunication by keeping everything in writing with an LOI. Although a LOI starts out as a letter from a buyer to a seller, don't be afraid to mark up the original letter or to write a response letter from the seller to the buyer with a counter-offer. The key to communication and how to avoid miscommunication with business deals is to put everything in writing.

If the offers are straight forward enough and don't require the resolution of any major issues besides price, then you can use purchase agreements to make offers. Either a buyer's agent or a buyer's attorney may draw up the agreement according to the terms of the buyer's offer and present a signed version of the agreement with a down payment check. Agreements are presented to sellers or their agents if they are represented by an agent. Down payment checks are normally written and presented to an attorney, a broker, or a title company to hold in an escrow account. Many agreements will allow down payment checks to be placed in escrow a few days after the agreement is signed by the seller, to avoid the escrow company from immediately having to refund a check if the deal is rejected. Once an offer is made, a seller may accept, reject, or counter the offer. Occasionally, they will do nothing. You can decide how to handle this, but in my experience, it is smart to assume the seller has rejected the offer. If a seller accepts the offer, the seller will sign the agreement and the down payment check gets presented to the escrowee to hold pending the completion of the closing or cancellation of the contract.

One note on purchase agreements, you may wonder why you should use an asset purchase agreement when businesses are owned by shareholders. Why not sell shares? The short answer is, sometimes businesses do, but research the law before you get involved in this. The federal government established rules through the Securities and Exchange Commission that regulates who can sell shares of a company and how those opportunities can be advertised. The federal courts have come out on both sides of the issue as to whether these SEC rules apply to privately-owned businesses and their brokers. The SEC does not regulate the sale of business assets where shares of a company are not exchanged, therefore to remain clear of any controversy, business owners and their brokers structure the deals as an asset purchase.

There is a bill going through Congress at this time—H.R.477 Small Business Mergers, Acquisitions, Sales, and Brokerage Simplification Act of 2017. The language of H.R. 477 has now been added as Title IX, Subtitle C of the 2019 Financial Services and General Government (FSGG) Appropriations Bill which is designed to exempt the brokering of shares of stock in privately-owned businesses without registering with the SEC. Furthermore, the SEC has already issued a no-action letter with regard to allowing unregistered brokers to sell shares of stock in privately owned companies. However, the scenario that the letter applies to is limited to the scope of that letter and may not apply to situations that an unsuspecting broker did not think of. My feeling for now is that you shouldn't advertise shares of stock or a percentage of a partnership for sale if you are representing a seller. If by some means you do get a buyer interested in a percentage of ownership, then have an attorney draw up the contract paperwork. This is usually done with a stock purchase agreement and attorneys are allowed to perform this work without an SEC license. Whether you are allowed to earn a commission on the transaction is still an issue to be determined. The main takeaway here is not to advertise or offer shares for sale which may draw governmental attention to your deal. On the other hand, if you are selling the assets, but a buyer decides to purchase the stock shares, that's your buyer's prerogative and you have not violated any SEC rules.

When submitting offers you should be very careful to submit offers respective of the deal. If you have ever heard the expression, the devil is in the details, it certainly applies to offers and contracts. It's so important that you read and know every detail before handing over written offers. One of the most common errors that I see is not attaching or obtaining an inventory accounting or list of assets. If that is not in the purchase agreement, it will remain an issue that must be worked out prior to closing. Many times, it becomes a point of contention at the closing and the attorneys or brokers involved cannot work out an amicable agreement. Another common issue is not agreeing to how long the seller is to stay during the transition period or how much he will be paid during an extended transition period. Without working these things out and putting them in the contract, your deals may go bust and you won't get paid. You shouldn't submit offers without your buyers knowing exactly what they are buying. Use an LOI if you need to work out issues prior to having your buyers enter contracts. Get everything in writing, dot your I's and cross your T's, and you will have a better closing rate than most agents.

Step-by-Step Guide

1. Every state has a different purchase agreement form to use for business purchases. Contact your local association of brokers, your broker, or a local business sales attorney for the proper form use to make offers.

2. Some cases may warrant the use of a proposal or LOI; otherwise, agents should try to use a purchase agreement to make offers due to the higher level of commitment it provides. At this stage, it is not referred to as an asset purchase agreement, it is called an offer to purchase.

   - Use a LOI when buyers are basing offers on conditions that need to be met.

   - You may also use an LOI to test out a lowball offer.

3. Call listing agents prior to presenting written offers and discuss the terms of the deal. Make your case and listen to feedback, then adjust the offers if necessary, if your buyers are still willing to negotiate.

4. When using a purchase agreement to make an offer, you may get a down payment from your buyer at the time of signing the agreement or allow for the down payment to be paid a few days after the offer is accepted and signed by the seller. The check should be made payable to the escrow agent "as escrowee."

5. Send the signed offer to the listing agent for their seller's signature. It is okay for one or both parties to use e-sign or fax if those are legal forms of signature in your state.

6. The seller may accept, reject, or counter the offer.

7. Make sure the purchase agreement is complete, including attached schedules of assets and inventory. If items are missing, create an addendum or have the buyer and seller get their attorneys to work out the issues as soon as possible. The more complete the agreement is in the early stages of the process, the better the chance of a successful deal later.

8. Do not advertise the shares of stock for sale. If a deal comes down to a stock sale, then have an attorney draw up the paperwork for the parties. The SEC has rules regarding the legality of this and the rules are still open to interpretation and have been used to violate unsuspecting business brokers.

Hiring an Attorney

Don't gain the world and lose your soul; wisdom is better than silver and gold. —Bob Marley

Since purchasing and selling businesses is legally intricate, buyers and sellers should be advised to hire an attorney to handle their transactions. That's advice from me with my attorney hat on. Likewise, buyers and sellers may hire accountants to handle due diligence, to form corporations, and to handle tax advice. In many states; however, business brokers handle the contract, the due diligence, and forming the new corporation, and an attorney or closing agent will handle the transfer papers and closing. After all, under the eyes of most state laws, business buyers are sophisticated investors and are expected to have a certain level of knowledge and experience that will allow them to avoid certain pitfalls that lay persons would not have seen. That said, most purchase agreements have a clause that allows buyers and sellers a certain amount of time to have an attorney review the contract without being bound to its terms until that time period expires. Each state has its own customs and laws regarding this matter. Furthermore, with respect to buyers and sellers using attorneys, some states will allow one attorney to handle both sides of a deal, while others treat deals as adversarial transactions and require that buyers and sellers each hire their own attorney.

With buyers, you should suggest that they use a good business sales attorney to complete their purchase. Most states work on the principal of caveat emptor (a legal doctrine summed up as, "buyer beware"), especially when it comes to business transactions, because buyers are considered sophisticated investors and are not afforded the same protections under the laws as consumers are. Aggrieved buyers may be out of luck trying to reverse deals and get their money back.

Now, some advice from me with my broker hat on—occasionally, buyers will use an attorney who is not experienced with business sales and closings. Usually, this attorney is a family member or friend. Nine times out of ten, this will kill the deal. Although the intentions are good, the results are usually disastrous. I remember one simple deal where the buyer's attorney took six months and billed his buyer client over $20,000 (some friend) only to have the buyer fire the attorney and hire me because his broker convinced him that his attorney was complicating the deal. I was able to read the paperwork, make a few changes, negotiate the changes with the seller's attorney and close the deal in three days at a cost of $1,500. Attorneys without experience in business closings or real estate transactions can cause so many delays and issues that the other side will cancel the deal. The delays and issues are a result of the attorney's lack of experience in the industry. Many attorneys, whether, corporate, criminal, or litigators, practice under adversarial conditions. On the other hand, business sales and real estate are theoretically fair transactions where each side bargains for their deal and then agrees to the terms upon signing the contract. The attorney's job should be to make sure the deal is completed as bargained for, which means that the sellers get their money and buyers get their assets. There isn't anything to advocate for at this point unless there is an inconsistency in the purchase agreement. If this happens, you should try to renegotiate it and resolve the issue. Adversarial attorneys, on the other hand, make issues out of everything; it's as if they are constantly trying to renegotiate entire deals to get their clients a better deal. That's not what the buyer and seller bargained for and that is not the type of counseling that is needed in business or real estate deals. The worst case is when the attorney is a corporate attorney or litigator but testing his skills at business sales. They bill by the hour. Even when these deals fall apart, the legal bill can be thirty or forty thousand dollars! Try to avoid this situation at all costs and advise your clients to use an experienced commercial real estate or transactional business attorney.

This may put you in a difficult situation because it's a sensitive discussion to have with clients, but the alternative is risking having your deals fall apart. Try counseling clients on the importance of choosing an experienced attorney and even recommending a reasonably priced attorney and explain that your brokerage has used that attorney multiple times without any issues. It's common for brokers to use the same closing attorneys to handle most of their deals and these attorneys will also take on representation of a buyer or seller if they are asked. The bottom line is that an inexperienced attorney will be a burden for a buyer or a seller and you should do your best to remedy this situation early on before the problems and legal bills start piling up. Depending on the size of the deal, you may even offer to pay for an attorney if your buyer is willing to make the change.

Step-by-Step Guide

1. Depending on the state you are in, the customs and laws will determine whether a buyer and seller have attorneys involved in the transaction or if the brokers handle the initial paperwork.

2. Some buyers will already have attorneys to handle the negotiation and/or the transaction regardless of state custom. Try to make sure these attorneys have transactional experience or do your best to replace them.

3. Whether the parties are represented or not, it is customary to have a closing agent handle the escrow money and the transaction paperwork. The closing agent can be an attorney or a title company.

4. Try to direct buyers and sellers to attorneys who have business sales experience. Your broker should have a list of attorneys who are available to handle business transactions.

Due Diligence and Pre-Closing Matters

If I don't learn something every single day, it's a wasted day. —Leonard Lauder

Due diligence is when buyers have the opportunity to review information about a business being purchased (usually financially related documents) in order to determine if the information provided to the buyer in the listing is correct. The asset purchase agreement will have a clause outlining the terms of the process. Buyers will normally have the right to cancel the purchase agreement if the information obtained in due diligence does not conform to the information in the listing. In fact, some agreements will allow buyers to cancel the agreement for almost any reason at all.

Purchase agreements will all differ on how to start the due diligence process. You should always read the agreement being used for your transaction to be mindful of the due diligence process. Most states have a standard agreement for business sales; however, some attorneys and brokers will not use those agreements or may change the due diligence clauses. These clauses can indicate that the process starts automatically on a certain date, that due diligence is waived, or that it starts upon some circumstance, such as, a buyer's written request. You will need to read each purchase agreement to know how to start the process and how long the buyer has to complete the process.

Normally, buyers may cancel a contract and receive their down payment back during the due diligence period. Once the due diligence period has past, buyers become locked into the contract. The industry term for this is, the money has gone hard, meaning that, after that date, buyers cannot get their down payment back under the terms of the due diligence clause. Of course, there may be other clauses in the agreement that allow the refund of a buyer's down payment, but the due diligence is most commonly the biggest hurdle to clear before getting the deal done.

Instead of due diligence, buyers may alternatively ask for an observation period. This means that buyers may go to a business and watch customers make purchases for a certain amount of time (normally a week or two, but possibly over a period of months). This procedure is used for businesses that take in a large amount of cash which doesn't show up in their financial statements or tax returns. The most common businesses that require an observation period are coin laundries, liquor stores, and bars. Generally, it only takes a week or two of observing because buyers should already have some idea of a business's revenue from other paperwork like purchase orders, electric or water bills, and bank statements or merchant accounts. The observation period is to verify the accuracy of their deduction from the con-temporaneous paperwork.

After due diligence is over or a buyer stipulates to ending it, there is a laundry list of matters for you to assist with in preparation for closing: franchisor approval, credit lines, lender approval (if there is a lender), licensure, vendors' or suppliers' agreements, an assignment of the lease or a new lease, transfer or opening a new merchant account, and an inventory accounting. You should stay in contact with the listing agent during this time and assist with coordinating all of these items. In other words, some of these items may be the responsibility of the seller, but both parties and their agents should coordinate efforts on all of the items to make sure everything gets done in a timely fashion.

The timing for all of these processes varies and you will need to go through it a couple of times to really understand each of them. Until then, you can plan to have your buyer finish due diligence before starting the other application processes, with the exception of the acquisition loan. The loan should be applied for immediately upon receiving a signed contract and you should continue to follow up to make sure the bank is working diligently on the process. With all of the other processes, you can make a phone call and get the applications, but don't bother applying until the due diligence is finished.

Franchise Approval

Franchisor approval (which is only necessary if your buyer is purchasing a new or existing franchise) refers to the process of buyers being vetted by the corporate company that owns the right to the franchise name. Let's say your client is buying an existing McDonalds, the buyer must meet certain financial qualifications, background qualifications, and then attend and pass a training class in order to be approved to purchase a McDonalds restaurant. Most contracts will be subject to the buyers obtaining franchise approval so the buyer can cancel the contract if it is not obtained.

Financing

Credit lines (or floorplans, as they are referred to in the vehicle sales industry) are the lines of credit used to operate a business. They are a line of credit for purchasing inventory, equipment, or for operating capital. For the most part, buyers must personally apply for new lines of credit through the same or different lenders. Normally, buyers will use the same lenders because the previous business track record may be taken into account for approval purposes. Many business credit lines are personally guaranteed by the owners; therefore, even if a buyer is buying a percentage of the existing business, that buyer may have to qualify and sign personally for any existing credit lines.

Business acquisition financing is generally in the form of SBA loans. Lenders will have paperwork for buyers and sellers after the contract is signed, but that won't be the end of it. A lender's representative may request a list of financial documents at any time and the requests seem to never end. And, just when you think the lender is ready and you will close, they will request more paperwork to make sure the financial situations of the buyer and sellers have not changed dramatically. Lenders seem to operate under the hurry up and wait concept; whereas, when they need something, they need it immediately, but most of the time they have no news and we are waiting for them to complete their underwriting process. Try to work with the same lenders over and over so you develop a relationship with the employees and are better able to get a handle on their particular process and the timing of everything. The entire loan process can be done in as little as two months, but I've seen it take as long as eight months.

Business Licensing

Licensure refers to your clients and their businesses obtaining the necessary licenses to operate. Sometimes, as in Florida, it can be as simple as mailing a check to the County with a one page form for a Business Tax Receipt; however, other businesses will need their sales tax licenses with the State, an occupancy license with the County; restaurants and food stores will need licenses from the Department of Health, some will need a liquor license; gas stations may need countless inspections with fire and zoning; and some businesses will need specific County or State licenses to operate in their particular industry, like a builder, a barber, an accountant, etc. These licenses sometimes apply to the individual owner, but others, like a health clinic license will apply to the business at each location. All of the different businesses that you sell will need different licenses depending their location. Each State and each County differ, so I can't teach you everything you need to know on this issue. It may take a few years to understand all of the important license requirements, so you should focus on the most common ones, such as, local municipal business licensing, liquor licensing, and zoning- fire and health (for food stores, restaurants, and bars). Be sure to work closely with each seller's agent to get your buyers qualified to do business before the closing. The best way to do this is to ask the seller what licenses and permits they need to operate and have your buyer apply for the same. In some cases, sellers may be willing to continue to qualify the businesses under their licenses while your buyers go through the application processes.

Suppliers

Vendors or suppliers are companies that sell inventory or operating supplies to businesses. Whether its gasoline for a gas station, groceries for a grocery store, or pizza boxes for a restaurant, these things get sold on a daily or weekly schedule and must be paid for. Some businesses pay C.O.D. but for the most part, these vendors give businesses terms, meaning that they have a certain amount of time to pay for the items. Since the terms are a form of credit, vendors require buyers to fill out an application and apply for their terms. Buyers can opt to pay cash for supplies, however, if the old business used vendor credit, then the new business will be operating under a different business model with different cash flow and may be risking a problem.

Premises Lease

The assignment of lease, if necessary, can be difficult and time consuming to obtain. The reasons it wouldn't be necessary is if the real estate were being sold to the buyers with the businesses, or if buyers were on purchasing a percentage of the company or shares in the company. If it is necessary, the you should start the process as soon as there is a signed purchase agreement. Ask the listing agent for the landlord's telephone number and if it is alright to start the approval process. Although it's generally the seller's responsibility to obtain the assignment, if the seller waits too long, it may delay the closing. Buyers need to apply for landlord approval as part of the assignment process, so you might as well just get the landlord's information and start the process as soon as you can. Some landlords have a lengthy approval process, or they may hire an attorney to draw up the paperwork. As you can imagine, if an attorney is involved, the process surely becomes lengthy. Attorneys can also be expensive and sometimes, landlords will charge the cost of the attorney to the seller (which should be stated in the seller's lease). Many leases have a fee amount for the transfer written into them and it is called an assignment fee. Supposedly, this is to pay for the assignment paperwork, but some of the fees are so high that they are a disincentive for smaller businesses to sell. The cost can become an issue between the parties, as most contracts are silent as to who covers this cost. In theory this is the sellers cost as you cannot sell a business if you can't transfer the business location to the buyer; however, since everything in business sales is negotiable, sellers will oftentimes try to get buyers to pay at least a portion of the fee.

If the lease is month to month or expiring shortly, the buyer may have to negotiate a new lease, rather than take an assignment of the existing lease. Some landlords will pay a commission to an agent for negotiating a new lease. If the buyer needs more space or to move the location, you should definitely try to negotiate a commission from the landlord, since this can be a time-consuming job for you. In general, the large multi-state property managers will pay a commission for this, but local landlords may not offer any compensation. Whether you are entitled to compensation under real estate laws is a question of facts and circumstance, so make sure you have an understanding with the landlord at the outset.

Merchant Account

If a business has retail clients, it probably has a merchant account, which means that the business accepts credit cards. Merchant accounts can be transferred from the seller to the buyer; however, most buyers prefer to set up a new account to avoid any confusion. Most banks have a merchant account service, or they have an affiliated company that they work with. Setting up a new account or transferring the old account is fairly simple and the merchant companies will assist buyers with this. The issue you will run into is how to change over the information on the exact day and time of closing. In other words, while everybody is at the closing table and for some time after that, the money may continue to go into the seller's bank account. Generally, there is a lag of a few days between when a transaction occurs and when the money gets deposited into the business bank account. To deal with this in a fair way, the closing agent can hold back some money in escrow to cover the few days of deposits that may go into the wrong bank account. The money is adjusted once the new merchant account is up and running correctly.

Business Inventory

The final inventory accounting needs to be arranged via appointment and is ordinarily done very close to the closing date. Sometimes this can be done by the buyer and seller by examining the inventory and analyzing the inventory tracking program. Otherwise, sellers will need an outside company to do this for them. If this needs to be done by an inventory company, then you need to schedule the inventory accounting in advance. Make sure the company is available when you need them because they get busy during certain times of the year and may need a lot of notice. There is a relatively small fee for this service that is usually paid by sellers.

Step-by-Step Guide

1. Purchase agreements will vary as to how due diligence starts, when it starts, and how long it lasts. Read each purchase agreement carefully to determine how to proceed with initiating and executing due diligence.

2. The usual document requests during the due diligence period include a copy of the lease, the franchise agreement (if any), profit and loss statements, tax returns, bank statements, purchase orders, vendor agreements, etc.

3. Your buyer may need an accountant to assist with auditing the requested documents during the due diligence process. Agents should be aware that any accountant will accept the job, but most accountants are unfamiliar with the specialty work needed. Accountants who are unfamiliar with the process may cause unnecessary issues and delays. It's best to locate an experienced business acquisition accountant through your local network of business brokers for this type of work.

4. If the buyer has requested an observation period instead of or in conjunction with due diligence, then read the agreement to determine how to initiate and execute that process.

5. If the business is a franchise, then you should arrange for your buyer to get a franchise application and go through the approval process.

6. The buyer and the business may have licenses that are needed in order to operate the business. Check with the seller to find out exactly what licenses

and permits are necessary.

7. Have your buyer apply for any necessary credit lines. Ultimately, it is up to your buyer whether he needs credit or not, but chances are that if the seller needed the credit, the buyer will too.

8. Send the lender a copy of the signed contract with the loan application and make sure that the approval process is proceeding forward. Keep following up every few days to track the progress until closing. Stay in contact with the bank representative because banks are notorious for dragging their feet.

9. Any vendors and suppliers should have an approval process. Some suppliers may require the buyer to put down a deposit, such as, a fuel supplier deposit for a gas station. The deposit may be as high as $200,000 and the approval process may take several weeks. For most vendors, there is a short application and a quick approval process.

10. If necessary, your buyer will need to apply for a new merchant account or transfer the existing merchant account. Either way, there is an application process and approval that should be initiated shortly after due diligence.

11. If your buyer is not purchasing the real estate, an assignment of the existing lease or a new lease is necessary to close the deal.

   - The seller is generally responsible for obtaining an assignment of the lease for the buyer; however, don't wait for the seller or his agent to start the process or it may delay the closing.

   - Work closely with the listing agent when dealing with the landlord and the lease.

   - The process isn't usually started until after due diligence is finished, but some landlords are notoriously slow, and the process should be started prior to that.

12. If a buyer is buying the land, then the land deal will be handled by a title company or attorney and you don't need a lease. Make sure that you have a contract for the sale of the land and that the title company is working on closing that deal simultaneously with the business sale.

   - If a buyer is purchasing real estate that is an integral part of the business, then your buyer should have two contracts with two separate down payments. The contracts are normally subject to and conditioned upon each other. They are usually closed simultaneously with the same closing agent.

13. Schedule an inventory accounting as necessary with the buyer and seller prior to the closing. If the seller maintains inventory trackable by computer program, then the buyer may review that inventory or have a third part company take

an accounting of the actual inventory on the shelves. If the business does not maintain an inventory program, then schedule an inventory company to do the accounting. You must schedule this in advance, so you don't delay the closing.

- The inventory being referred to here is for product-based industries, like, distributors or groceries. If the industry is service-based but maintains inventory in order to produce a service, like, a window contractor, then you will probably not use an inventory accounting company. The accounting company is generally used to barcode scan retail products rather than to count screws and nails.

- With service-based companies, their clients will pay a deposit for the company to purchase supplies prior to initiating service, therefore, their value is not calculated by the amount of product purchased but in the amount of services or service hours produced. Alternatively, a product-based company spends its own money to purchase supplies and turns them over at a higher price. Their entire profit and therefore value is based on the amount of product they turn over each month. Hence, an inventory accounting is applicable to the value of the product-based company.

14. Follow up with the closing attorney and listing agent until the closing date to help work out any issues. There is almost always legwork to do, so stay on top of things in order to keep the deal together and moving towards the closing.

Working with Buyers Who Need a U.S. Visa

Doing the best at this moment puts you in the best place for the next moment.
—*Oprah Winfrey*

There are two types of investors' visas available to international business buyers, the E2 and the EB5 visas. As of 2018, there are plenty of serious international business buyers who contact business brokers each year looking to gain citizenship through the EB5 visa program. Yet, there are 10,000 visas available each year in the U.S. and some go unused. Alternatively, the E2 investors visa is cheaper and faster to acquire but the main drawback is it is temporary rather than permanent.

To understand how the EB5 program works, you should first understand the E2 visa. The E2 visa is a temporary visa for up to five years and is renewable. In order to qualify, a foreign investor needs to invest $100,000 in a US based business, be actively involved in management, produce enough income to support his family, and generate or maintain one or two jobs for U.S. workers. There is also the requirement that investors maintain at least a 50 percent ownership in the company(ies) if two owners, or 51 percent if more than two owners. The time frame to obtain an E2 visa is approximately 30-60 days for a qualified applicant.

Another caveat is that E2 investors may only be from treaty countries. A list of current treaty countries can be found on the United States Customs and Immigration Service website.

The EB5 visa, on the other hand, is a path to citizenship: investors are issued green cards initially, and eventually may apply for citizenship. It normally takes about one year for the visa to be issued and requires a minimum investment of $500,000 or $1,000,000 depending on the location of the business ($500,000 in a targeted employment area). EB5 Investors must create ten new jobs, net enough income to support their families each year, possess the qualifications necessary to run the businesses, and actively participate in management. The treaty country caveat does not apply to the EB5 visa, so, the investor can be from any country in the world except North Korea (currently).

Since the E2 visa takes 30-60 days to obtain and the EB5 may take a year, it's logical that investors will apply for the E2 visa first, whether the business qualifies for the EB5 or not. This gives the investor five years of legal status to work in the US. Once that visa is obtained and the business has been purchased, the investor can "upgrade" and apply for the EB5 visa. Coincidentally, the investment amount is cumulative and can be spread across different businesses. This means that, investors may start by purchasing one gas station worth $100,000 and continually purchasing other gas stations or any other type of business that they wish until they have invested a cumulative $1,000,000 to qualify for the EB5 visa.

The investment visa process is ambiguous to say the least, and a good immigration attorney is an integral part of the visa process for investors. Business brokers will routinely advertise that their listings will qualify buyers for visas; however, that determination cannot be made without the assistance of an attorney who deals with visa applicants. Whether a buyer has the required experience to run the business, and whether the business will net enough money to support the applicant and his family as required by our immigration rules needs to be evaluated by an immigration attorney. It is absolutely necessary for buyers looking for an investor's visa to retain an immigration attorney prior to working with you. If not, they are wasting your time by requesting information on businesses that may not qualify. You absolutely have no idea which businesses will qualify for which buyers. The only way to obtain this information is through an immigration attorney. By the way, a clean criminal record is also a requirement. How many of your buyers allow you to do a background check on them before you start working with them? Again, until you have all of this information, don't waste your time working with foreign buyers. Send them to an immigration attorney who you have developed a working relationship with so that the attorney can prequalify these candidates for you.

Step-by-Step Guide

1. As a condition to applying for an investors visa, buyers need to enter into a

contract to purchase a business.

2. The E2 visa takes about 30-60 days to obtain and the EB5 may take a year or longer.

3. Foreign investors need to invest a cumulative amount of at least $100,000 for the E2 visa and $1,000,000 for the EB5 visa. The E2 visa may only be obtained by investors from a treaty country.

4. A qualifying business must produce enough income for a buyer and a buyer's family to live on. We don't know exactly what that means, so you will want to contact an immigration attorney for help qualifying buyers and businesses.

5. Buyers cannot have a criminal record.

6. Develop a working relationship with a good immigration attorney so you can refer buyers to the attorney and get feedback as to whether a buyer will qualify and for which businesses.

7. Foreign buyers without an attorney should contact an immigration attorney, get a consultation, and pay a retainer fee. If a buyer refuses to do that, consider that buyer unqualified and not serious. It's up to you what to do with your buyers, but I advise you not to waste your time.

8. A typical way to obtain citizenship under the investors visa program is for foreign investors from a treaty country to enter into a purchase contract and apply for the E2 visa. This is done whether buyers want an EB5 visa or not. If they qualify for the EB5 visa, they can apply for that visa while legally in the US on an E2 visa. The caveat is that only buyers from treaty countries can get an E2 visa.

9. Due to the number of foreign investors in Florida, it is common for sellers to reject purchase agreements that are conditioned on investors receiving a visa. It is more common for the investors to take the risk and enter contracts that are not conditioned on receiving a visa. Many times, investors will ask for a 30-day due diligence period to limit this risk. Local immigration attorneys have become so adept at the process that they are able to tell their clients if they are likely to qualify for the visa of not. Perhaps many foreign investors are worried about the current administration and the tightening of immigration standards. I've personally known one buyer who have had to leave the country after being rejected for the visa. Fortunately, he had family here to run the business and sell it for him after he left.

10. Investors who are not from treaty countries may only apply for the EB5 visa, which entails entering into a contract to purchase a business conditioned upon the visa after one year. This is unlikely to happen for two reasons: First, sellers won't agree to hold their businesses off the market for one year while the in-

vestor applies for the visa. Second, investors can get an EB5 visa by investing $500,000 in an approved EB5 center. Centers are large real estate projects that are funded by hundreds of EB5 investors. The money is invested for 10 or 15 years and then returned with little or no interest, but they are eligible for the visa once the money is paid.

• For this reason, I have never heard of investors not being from treaty countries who were able to get an EB5 visa.

Working with Buyers Who Need Financing

I try to skate to where the puck is going to be, not where it is at the moment.
—Wayne Gretzky

Buyers can be prequalified for a business acquisition loan; however, the loan will be conditioned on the ultimate approval of a particular business. This means that the buyer and the business must meet certain financial qualifications. The Small Business Administration (SBA) is the government entity that backs business acquisition loans (and other business financing) which are provided by lenders (banks and private lenders). The process is very simple, and the loans are generally based on the cash flow of a business with a little or no emphasis on the balance sheet. These loans can be used to cover up to 85percent of the purchase price and can be used to pay for goodwill. The lending banks may also give buyers working capital loans at closing which can effectively bring the financing up to 100percent of the purchase price. This does not mean that buyer without any money can buy a business, the buyers must be able to meet underwriting criteria, which normally entails the buyer having at least 15percent of the purchase price in cash available for the purchase. The SBA is a great tool for business brokers and, as an agent, you should frequently try to qualify buyers for SBA loans.

Some businesses are difficult to finance because they don't show much profitability on their tax returns (i.e., some coin laundries may not report all of their cash revenue). Some businesses may have other impediments to obtaining financing; for example, check cashing stores are considered risky due to regulatory constraints. Alternatively, sometimes it's the buyers who cannot qualify for a particular company due to inexperience in that industry. Lenders will look at all of the important criteria in order to evaluate their risk when determining whether or not they will make the loan.

The SBA does have standard criteria that lenders have to work with for loan approvals, but lenders sometimes impose added criteria. In other words, lenders cannot write SBA loans unless they meet the SBA criteria, but lenders can choose not to write a loan based on their preferences for loans in certain industries. Lenders differ with their criteria for loans and you should shop around to find out what each lenders criterion is. Introduce yourself to at some local SBA lenders and become familiar with their loan approval processes. Many times, loan officers will take you out to lunch or provide you with a seminar on how to get your buyers and sellers approved for SBA loans through their company. In my experience private lenders have more leeway with financial criteria and will lend to more industries than banks. That said, I've found that buyers feel more comfortable dealing with banks than with private lenders even though private lenders may have more competitive interest rates or fees.

There are other sources of financing and acquisition strategies besides the SBA that may be implemented by buyers, namely, inventory loans, operating capital loans, hard money loans, equity investors and seller financing. It's even possible to pair up a few compatible buyers to purchase a business as a partnership if this makes for a more qualified buyer. Perhaps the buyers can't get a loan individually, but together they may. This would be unusual but not impossible. Bank financing is great when you are able to use it, but don't rely on it for the primary source of deal funding. It is important for you to develop a network and a familiarization with the resources and strategies in order to become a deal maker. Every deal is not a cash deal or a straightforward purchase with SBA financing. Many deals are a combination of partnerships, outside financing, and seller financing.

As a new agent, you should look to grow a network that consists of different lenders, other agents, equity investors, attorneys, accountants, and business owners. In fact, most deals are not done with traditional bank financing, most deals are done with a combination of different sources of financing and some innovative thinking. Good agents will learn to use their network and to think outside of the box. Agents who pass on deals where buyers come up short on money, will give up a lot in the long run. Every deal that gets done is not only a commission for now, but a referral for the future: Buyer's become sellers someday, buyers also may leverage up and make other acquisitions using the profit from the business they just bought. This is referred to as your pipeline and it can only grow when it is fed. Making deals happen is the best and quickest way to feed your pipeline.

One quick word about hard money lenders: they will want to be paid points up front (3 to 6 points), a high interest rate (maybe 12-18 percent or more) and offer short loan terms (three years at most). This is an expensive price to pay, but in some circumstances, the loans can be used as a bridge loan. It might be of use to buyers who expect to be able to pay off the loan in a short period of time.

By and far, seller financing is the most common form of financing used on small business deals. It is simple to arrange, and the rate and terms are negotiable. In fact, many buyers will insist on seller financing in order to limit their risk when buying a business. Sellers on the other hand, are not usually enthusiastic about seller financing because they have to wait for their money and are taking the risk that the money will never come if their buyer goes out of business to no fault of the seller's. At the end of the day, many deals are completed with some seller financing because sellers who give financing are much more likely to sell in the end and sell their business for a higher price than sellers who do not provide financing.

Step-by-Step Guide

1. About 75 percent of all transactions are accomplished with some type of financing.

2. Financing may take anywhere from a few days to eight weeks, depending on the type of financing involved: An SBA loan will take about 60 days, most other financing can be done in two weeks or less.

3. Try to get all buyers prequalified for financing. This entails having your buyers speak with a SBA lender and filling out any pre-qualification paperwork necessary. The formal SBA loan application process cannot be started until a prospective business is identified. This has to do with SBA underwriting restrictions about approving or denying buyers within a certain time limit. However, most lenders and loan brokers can start a pre-qualification process at any time. Most lenders will give buyers a verbal verification, but some will issue them a pre-qualification letter. This will help you weed out the tire kickers so that you only deal with serious buyers.

4. Alternatively, you can find a loan broker to work with and send your buyers to that broker. The broker can do all of the pre-qualification and applications paperwork with your buyers, so you can focus on selling businesses.

5. Even when buyers get approval for SBA loans, the businesses will also have to qualify based on cash flow or sometimes by showing asset valuations. Since the businesses are usually being approved on cash flow, buyers with poor credit are not a deal breaker. It's always worth having a conversation with lenders when buyers are worried about their credit score, this is something that can be overcome.

    •   Conventional business acquisition loan financing through the SBA has the strictest criteria and takes longer to get approval than loans through hard money lenders; however, the trade-off is that SBA lenders have much better rates and terms.

    •   Seller financing is the simplest way to get the money that buyers need. The terms are negotiable and generally much better than hard money loans.

    •   Sometimes it's possible to use a combination of multiple types of financing. The SBA sometimes allows limited seller financing to be used in conjunction with SBA loans.

6. Occasionally, you will find that there is no way to make a deal work. But you

still have to try. Don't just drop a buyer if a lender says no. There are lenders for every level of risk, there are investors, other partners, or other deals that can be made. Think outside of the box and try to work your magic. When there is a will, there is a way. This is very difficult before you have experience, but you need to start trying different possibilities to develop your network and skillset that will pay off for you on deals that come to you later in your career.

Assisting Buyers with Franchises

The more you learn the more you earn. —Robert Dedman

A franchise business is set up with a contract to do business under a corporate name between the franchisor (corporate owner) and the franchisee (local business owner). If the business owner wishes to sell the business, the buyer and seller must look to the terms of the franchise agreement to determine how to sell the business and what costs must be paid to the franchisor. Furthermore, franchise agreements give franchisors the right to approve prospective buyers. Franchisors want to protect the integrity of their corporate names by having owners with strong financials and qualified business backgrounds operating their franchises. This helps assure the franchisors that the franchisees will be successful.

Normally franchise agreements will specify any franchise transfer fees that are to be paid to the franchisors upon the sale or transfer of the franchisees' businesses. The fee or fees are charged to sellers, but many times sellers will add the fee to the price of their business and ask buyers to pay the fee. A franchise fee can be anywhere from a few thousand dollars to more than $300,000, depending on the desirability of the franchise. Normally, the fee is not negotiable, but I have seen cases where it was reduced by a franchisor in order to complete a deal. Branding is important to franchise companies and it's better for them to have locations stay in business than to close.

Franchise agreements may include monthly or quarterly payments to the franchisor for advertising fees and revenue sharing. This is important information for buyers because it shows how much of their gross revenue the business will have to share with the franchisor. The agreement also contains the rules by which the franchisee must operate. Things like minimum square footage of leases, lease locations, number of employees and training of employees are just some of the things that are specified in the franchise agreements. For all of these reasons, it is important that buyers have access to franchise agreements prior to entering into purchase agreements with sellers.

Step-by-Step Guide

1. Franchised businesses have agreements in place that give franchisors the right

to approve buyers.

- Besides having an application process, sometimes franchisors have training classes or even tests for buyers to pass.

- Buyers must obtain and read a copy of any franchise agreement before purchasing a franchise business. The agreement may be obtained before making the offer, but absolutely must be obtained in due diligence.

2. Franchise agreements can affect the purchase agreement with conditions that must be met by buyers and sellers.

3. Most franchise agreements contain a transfer fee that must be paid upon transfer or sale of the business. This fee must be negotiated by the buyer and seller prior to entering into a purchase agreement. Although sellers are responsible to pay the fee to their franchisor, they often try to pawn the fees off as a buyer's expense.

4. Get a copy of the franchise agreement and speak to the listing agent about any anomalies that you might encounter with the franchise. It is a good idea to make a list of requirements and fees that are involved to assist a buyer with reviewing the franchised business.

Sample Buyer Spiel

There is little difference in people, but that little difference makes a big difference. That little difference is attitude. The big difference is where it is positive or negative. —Clement Stone

As a new agent, it is understandable that you will feel intimidated about speaking with buyers and afraid of saying the wrong thing. This is part of the learning curve and there really is only one cure: You need to talk to buyers, a lot of buyers. You will make mistakes and you will get better at it very quickly. In the meantime, here is a sample spiel to study to help you get over your stage fright and feel more comfortable about the process.

If there is one thing that you should remember it is to make friends with buyers. If they like you, they will use you as their agent. It's really that simple.

- Hello, Mr. Buyer, this is {your name} from {your company name} calling you about the gas station that you inquired about. How can I help you?

- Can I give you some immediate general information about that listing before I send you an NDA to sign? (i.e. general location, net or gross sales, reason for selling, etc.)

- Does this sound like something that you would be interested in or would you like me to find something [in a different area, easier to run, with a higher net, etc.]?

- Do you have criteria for a business that you are looking for or did you just start looking for a business to buy?

- How much money do you have available to put as a down payment, so I know how to limit my search?

- If you want, I can help you get prequalified for a business acquisition loan. We work with lenders and brokers who you can speak with over the telephone to find out if you qualify. It will only take about ten minutes of your time.

- What is your background or industry experience?

- May I please have your name, address, and email so I can send you a NDA to sign, and then I can give you more information on this opportunity?

- Okay, I will send you the NDA to sign and when I receive it back signed, I will email you the listing sheet along with some other information about the business. Also, if you would like to see the business, I would be happy to arrange a showing or a telephone call with the seller.

- *Next call...* Hi Mr. Buyer, I was calling to follow up on the information that I sent you and to see if you had any questions [pick a subject... about the lease terms, about the current manager and employees, about the gross sales or net benefit to owner, about the owner's daily routine, about regulatory compliance, about the franchise agreement, etc.]?

- If you aren't sure about that listing, maybe you would like to look at this other business that is for sale; it's about the same price but [use any benefits of the other business here... i.e. has a higher owner's benefit or might be easier to finance].

CHAPTER 6

Working with Sellers

A long apprenticeship is the most logical way to success. The only alternative is overnight stardom, but I can't give you a formula for that. —Chet Atkins

Accelerated Learning Tip

Take as many courses and seminars as you can during your first and second year. Most business broker associations offer free or discounted courses to their members.

Real-Life Experience

Develop a niche by selecting an industry to work in. I never did. I managed agents working in every industry for most of my career and developed knowledge about each industry. Now I'm a jack of all trades but master of none. If I had it to do over again, I'd select restaurants. In south Florida, there are more restaurants per square mile than almost anywhere in the world. Consequently, restaurants account for more than a third of all businesses sold each year in Florida.

Preparation for a Listing Appointment

Just as with buyers, it's important to distinguish what you are selling to prospective business sellers: A good business broker is selling an exit strategy for business owners, or more specifically, a system by which sellers can retire, liquidate, free up time, or move on to another venture. With that in mind, you should remember that to obtain a listing, you will need to understand what each seller is trying to achieve and provide them with the right opportunity to obtain that goal.

Preparation is paramount to a successful listing presentation. Sellers need to be prepared for it as well. You should advise them that you will need about 45 minutes of their time and it would be nice if they have financial information available while you're there. They should also have their key person in charge available if that person is aware of the sale. Sometimes this is not possible because sellers don't always want to tell employees they are selling. In either case, you should prepare yourself and your sellers prior to initial meetings. You should use a checklist that you can email to sellers ahead of time that describes how you operate as a broker and what information you will need. A checklist can really give sellers an idea of how complex and time consuming the business sale process is, which can help weed out the sellers who are not serious about selling but only interested in a valuation. These are the sellers who call you after they just spoke to a friend who got a good price for their business and are fishing to see if they can bring in such a large price. Don't get me wrong, everybody wants a valuation, especially prior to selling, but if they are not willing to put time in to the process, then they will not be willing to put the larger amount of time in that selling requires.

Most of your competition is not very organized and they will go to listing presentations with very little information to offer except what is on their minds. You shouldn't work this way and will find that if you do, you may wind up with a lot of listings that are difficult to sell. Agents who are good talkers and are able to get sellers to sign a listing agreement are rarely the most successful listing agents. In fact, don't go to your initial meetings equipped to get a signed listing agreement. Don't even bring one with you. If a seller asks for one, then you can always email it later, but rarely do they ask. Think of listings as a multi-step process. The first meeting is about judging if you want to take the listing or not. If you feel that the seller has a sellable business and you feel that you can work well with the seller, then take the listing. If that happens, then you can start to educate the seller on how the entire sales process works. There will be plenty of time to get the listing agreement signed. The listing process can take anywhere from 20 to 200 hours of work, and the sales process can take years.

Slow Down and Do Things the Right Way

Education is the key to gaining sellers' trust. Trust is essential to gaining listings. Think of the initial meeting as a therapy session where you will listen at first and then introduce sellers to how to seller their businesses. Just as most buyers are first-time buyers, most sellers are also first-time sellers and they have never done this before. When it's your turn to speak and you are ready to start educating your seller, make sure to start with the big picture in mind before going into details; keep the conversation general and slowly introduce details.

Sellers always want to steer the conversation towards valuation and how much they can get for their businesses, so I usually start there. I'll say something like, "in order to determine valuation, we first need to determine who our target buyer is and how much money the buyer has." From there, I'll elaborate on the fact that different buyers are willing to pay different amounts for businesses and identify the three different types of buyers as competitors, income buyers, and equity funds. In fact, most competitors will pay less than most income buyers, which usually surprises sellers.

Knowing the target buyer will help us understand how much financing a buyer might need. Generally, competitors and equity funds are cash buyers, however, sometimes equity funds will require some seller financing. All this information and more is part of a business valuation report. Eventually, the information from the report gets put into a memorandum for buyers to see and evaluate the business with. Explaining the process to sellers helps them understand that a business valuation is much more complex and time consuming than just tossing out a multiple of earnings and listing the business for that number.

I also like to discuss the listing process and how long it can take, including an explanation of the marketing and advertising I plan to do. The conversation can be lengthy but when you just start out, you'll likely be working with smaller businesses and you won't have to go into so many details. The smaller the business, the simpler the issues. You can simplify the process until you've gone through it a couple of times and are really able to speak about it in detail.

In fact, let the sellers do most of the talking. Sellers don't want to be sold, they want to feel comfortable with the agent representing them. This means that you have to listen to what sellers are trying to accomplish and make sure you tell them that you can provide what they need. Once you have some experience, you can make a portfolio of prior sales and some testimonials to boost your position, but until then, just keep things simple and lead them towards the fact that you can help them accomplishing their goal. The formula to gaining listings is to listen, educate, and lead sellers to gain their trust.

The first step towards getting a listing has traditionally been to have sellers sign a listing agreement and commit to working with you. Alternatively, you can choose to use two agreements: a retainer agreement before evaluating a business, and a marketing agreement after the valuation is done. This is something that you can explore to see what works best for you. Since, getting a signed listing agreement won't happen until you've gained a seller's trust. For this reason, it makes more sense to use a retainer agreement before evaluating a business, and then use a signed authorization to market the business once the business has been evaluated and the asking price has been established.

At this point, you can show sellers how you will evaluate their businesses by going through your procedure and checklist with then. Explain that doing an evaluation requires that you will act like a buyer to evaluate their business from a buyer's perspective. This should make perfect sense to them. In any case, you can show them the listing information worksheet. The information worksheet is a questionnaire that asks sellers about every aspect of their businesses. You can go over the questionnaire with sellers or you can ask them to fill it out over the next few weeks. Most sellers will ask you for your assistance with the worksheet. This is generally a good idea, but some sellers are diligent with paperwork and can do a good job by themselves. It may take two or three return trips before you receive all of the information that is need; coincidently, it may take that many times for sellers to become comfortable enough with you to sign a listing agreement. Sometimes sellers withhold a listing agreement until they see that you are working diligently on their listing worksheet or until you have come up with a valuation for them.

Once you have all the necessary paperwork and information, you can provide a business valuation for your sellers. Make sure you present this in-person at a meeting. Many times, sellers like to meet at their place of business, but the meeting can be at a local coffee shop or at your office. Your valuations may consist of many suggestions about business improvements. In other words, you should try to pick out the positives and negatives of each business, show sellers how their businesses compare to other similar businesses, and what they can do to increase the value of their businesses. This may cause quite a few sellers each year to decide not to sell but instead to use your value enhancement recommendations. Don't worry about this. You won't lose all of these listings. In fact, those clients will return in a few months and become your best sales. If they were willing to do everything you suggested to enhance their businesses (which is their livelihood), then many times, they will come back in a year or less and have doubled their business values. And when they return, there is no more sales pitch necessary, it's like you have become best friends at that point. They are ready for you to sell their businesses with full confidence.

A famous person once said that you have to be the person you want to become. In other words, if you want to become a highly successful business broker, then you must start doing the things that highly successful business brokers do: The best business brokers are great counselors and consistently counsel their sellers on how to maximize the value of their businesses before selling them. This makes for higher business sales prices, but also makes the businesses more sellable; therefore, they are selling businesses for higher prices in less time than other brokers.

Some listing appointments start out as free business valuations, which are commonly offered by brokers as a way of prospecting for sellers. Treat these prospects as actual clients rather than prospective clients. To help you do this, you should think of what you would do if they were you're your businesses. When doing valuations, try to advise sellers of what can be done to increase the value of their businesses. This way, they can focus on bringing their business values up as high as possible prior to committing to selling.

Be sure to keep in touch with prospective sellers: try to stop by every month or so and talk about recent transactions or show them listings of new similar businesses. Keeping in touch with prospects has been shown to increase sales dramatically as compared to just waiting for them to callback. The time and money were already spent on these prospects, they are the most familiar with your and willing to talk to you, so don't lose them by not following up.

Another thing to remember is that listing appointments should be scheduled when employees and customers are not around. Most sellers don't want anybody to know their businesses are for sale: They are afraid of losing clients, employees, contracts, or accounts. This makes it difficult to meet during business hours. If employees are around when you go to visit, you should introduce yourself as a business consultant or some other job title that does not alert them to your real purpose. Keep this in mind, as there is no better way to lose a listing than to walk in and say that you are a business broker here to meet with the seller.

How to Achieve Greatness as a Business Broker

Selling businesses is a better business model than selling buyers businesses because being in control of business listings means being in control of your source of income. If you list a certain number of businesses each month, you should sell a certain percentage of those listings. Occasionally, you should get both commission sides of a deal, which doesn't happen to buyer brokers, and you can sell a prospective buyer a completely different listing. By listing businesses, you are creating a pipeline that you can rely on for income. Buyers agents don't have that. They need to compete for buyers with other agents, hope the buyers buy through them and don't leave, and waste time with too many buyers who are just looking. Some agents do well working buyers. Those agents tend to have a niche: maybe they only work restaurants or franchises, but by maintaining a niche, they already know what their buyers are looking for and they already have some good matches for them through their existing contacts. The fact remains that, by and far, the most successful agents in the industry are selling businesses and not selling buyers businesses.

Don't get discouraged if at first, you don't get every listing you try for, in fact, after you get some experience, you won't want every listing because you will see that some sellers are difficult to work with and some businesses are not worth what their sellers are demanding for them. You should try to work only with sellers that you feel are being honest and businesslike, and with businesses that you think you can sell. Honesty is important because if sellers are lying to you it may not only make you look bad in front of buyers and other brokers, but it can be a liability for you from a fraudulent standpoint. Remember that you will have to make some representations to buyers and you can be liable for your words. Trust but verify, and if you find that a seller is lying, don't take that listing for any reason.

Another way to achieve greatness is to establish a niche within an industry. Most successful brokers have a niche which allows them to create a network within that industry. A network will help get you more listings, larger listings, and to complete more deals. To establish your niche, you need to market the industry to pick up buyers and sellers in that industry. It will take some time and effort, but after a year or two, things will become easier as your network grows.

In the following chapters you will go through the process of listing and selling businesses. Most business brokers do not operate with the same procedure as far as preparation and thoroughness of business listings. You will notice that they will take many more shortcuts and they don't put great effort into their listing process. Their methodology is to post as many listings as they can and hope they sell a lot of them. This doesn't work as well. Business brokers on average sell 22 percent of their listings. On the other hand, if you employ the following process: gain almost every detail available about how a business operates, compare it to other similar business, point out benefits and detriments of ownership, make suggestions about how to overcome those detriments, display those detriments as opportunities to buyers, suggest a target category of buyers and show why, arrange prequalified financing, show why a business is priced the way it is, suggest different sales prices based on offers with SBA financing, seller financing, and a cash price. These things take time to figure out and to write down in a report. They take facts and figures, and justification of how you compare those facts and figures. At the end of the day, you need to feel confident in your work and your research and sell that information to your sellers and then to your buyers. This is very different from throwing up listings at a price suggested by the sellers and asking buyer what they would like to pay. I know based on my personal experience that if you follow the procedure outlined in the next few chapters, your payoff at the end of the year should be a sales ratio of more than 85 percent compared to 22 percent. Remember that 22 percent is the average ratio. Most brokers only sell one listing and some won't sell any each year.

CHAPTER 22

Procedure When Working with Sellers

Answer your Phone! Or, Call Sellers Immediately Upon Receiving a Lead

...my duty is a thing I never do, on principle. —Oscar Wilde

Sellers are looking for a competent business professional to counsel and advise them through the successful sale of their businesses. To be professional, you must telephone sellers immediately upon receiving their calls or emails. Make appointments to meet them in person. Do not text or email sellers: Texts and emails are an impersonal way to communicate and you need to develop a personal rapport with sellers in order to gain their trust and to get their listings.

Don't worry if sellers can't have financial documents available at the first meeting, just set up the initial meeting to introduce yourself. It's important to meet with sellers as soon as possible while you have their attention. Waiting more than a few days to meet may allow sellers to become distracted with running their businesses and it may be difficult to get another appointment.

It may be difficult to get a meeting with sellers because they are weary of contacting a broker and being sold something they don't want. They are thinking that you are only after their listing without regard for their best interests. This will change of course as you earn their trust, but during the initial telephone call, sellers will not trust you. Remember that a seller's purpose of a call is to find out how much their business is worth, and your purpose is to get a meeting with the seller. The two purposes are not necessarily conflicting, but you'll need to be prepared to delay the seller's purpose until after you've achieved your purpose. If you were to break down and give the seller an off-the-cuff valuation on the telephone, then you are not as likely to get your meeting and therefore have decreased your chances of a sale.

During a call, you should expect the owner to ask how much the business is worth. Your response can be something like this, "I'd be happy to meet with you to learn more about your business and how you operate it, so I can create a detailed valuation report for you. The valuation will take about two weeks for me to complete but there is no obligation for you to sell. Do you have time to meet tomorrow?"

Occasionally owners will push back a little bit at this point and say that they just want to know what percentage of income we use so they can see if their business is worth selling. In other words, they just want an answer now over the telephone. Until and unless you can get in front of business owners, get their full attention, and provide them with a complete valuation that you can explain and justify, any valuation that you give them over the telephone will sound like too small of an amount to them, so don't waste your time. An owner that pushes back and won't give you your meeting is not likely to become a client.

At the meetings, you should expect to outline the sales process procedure for sellers but let them do the talking at first. Seller's don't want to be sold with a sales pitch. They are looking for a confidant who can listen to what their needs are and guide them through the process on how to obtain their goals. For them to allow you to guide them, you need to win their trust by listening to what they need, and then, advising them that you have the process in place to get them to their goals. Some sellers will try to have this conversation on the telephone to avoid the meeting. They will ask how you value and sell businesses. Tell them you need a half hour of their time to lay the entire process out for them and would like to set the meeting for tomorrow if they are available. Your goal on the telephone is to get a meeting. Without a meeting, you won't win their trust and you won't get their listing.

When making appointments with sellers, you must be persistent, but don't be annoying. Remember that you should present yourself as a competent business professional. When sellers don't respond, it means that they are likely busy running their businesses. Be patient and put their contacts on your calendar to follow up in a few days or weeks. Many agents put sellers on an e-newsletter list or a monthly email drip to keep in front of their prospects. This is something that you can do on your own if you like to write articles and are tech savvy or you can subscribe to a service that will assist you with it. Business Brokerage Press and Newsletter Station are two of the common newsletters used for keeping in touch with clients.

Step-by-Step Guide

1. Answer your telephone as much as possible so you don't miss calls from sellers.

2. Telephone sellers immediately upon receiving a voicemail or email, don't rely on email or text. Email and text are impersonal ways to communicate. You need to establish personal contact and develop a business relationship to gain sellers' trust.

3. Always ask to see sellers' businesses at the next available appointment. A good technique to use with hesitant sellers is to ask to see the business because you deal with buyers daily and you may just run across the perfect buyer for their business. This is a great way to get your foot in the door, so you can eventually get the listing. The more personal contact you have with sellers, the stronger the rapport will become.

4. Try not to value businesses over the telephone. Sellers may not like or understand the valuation and it's easy to say no over the phone. Your entire purpose of the telephone call is to get a listing appointment.

5. Getting listings is all about trust and relationship. Try to develop a relationship over the telephone and then in person to gain sellers' trust. This may be done in one meeting or over the course of several meetings.

    - First, get to know sellers.

    - Next, get to know their businesses.

    - Ask questions and then listen to what they say. Respond appropriately and try to keep them talking: The more sellers talk, the more comfortable they will become and the better the chances of you getting meetings and listings.

6. Sometimes sellers call several different agents to interview. Don't worry about this. Just stick to your normal routine and keep following up until you get a clear "yes or no." It's like playing golf against an opponent: To win, you need to play against the course, not the opponent. Find out what sellers need and try to offer that service. Education is the best method to use. If you can educate sellers, then they will trust you. Don't worry about what other agents say or do, just focus on your game.

7. Be persistent and keep in touch with prospects. You can also stop by to see sellers and bring them comparable sales information. Be persistent but not annoying and hopefully when the time is right, you will get an appointment.

Evaluate Whether You Want the Listing or Not

As a rule, he or she who has the most information will have the greatest success in life.
—Benjamin Disraeli

Entice sellers to talk about their businesses so you can see if you want to take their listings. It's fairly easy to do, you simply say, "Tell me about your business and why you want to sell." Some sellers will go on for 45 minutes without taking a break. If they don't get to the important topics, then lead them a little, "Tell me about how you generate sales?" or "What are your duties in the company?" or "What are your plans after you sell?" These questions will lead to more talking, and they will give you insight into whether the company has value or not.

Why wouldn't you want every listing? There are a few reasons, the first and most important is that you won't get along with every seller. If you can't form a team with a seller and have a good working relationship, then the listing will be difficult, time consuming, and frustrating. The second is that not every business is sellable at the price a seller is willing to take. If sellers are not reasonable about pricing businesses, then you shouldn't waste your time.

When I first started out, I listed a liquor store where the seller said he had $1 million in inventory and he would accept $1 million for the business. I thought he was being generous and got excited about the possibility of making my first $100,000 commission. I eventually found a buyer and got the business into contract, but the buyer's accountant discovered during due diligence that the seller was moving his inventory to a bar he owned selling it there. He wasn't booking it, which means that he was trying to inflate his inventory prior to the sale. The buyer wanted the store anyway and offered a reasonable price of $300,000, but the seller refused saying that he knows the store is worth $1 million. Well, I lost that buyer and then the next buyer. After six months, I finally wised up and told him I'm not working for him anymore. As it turns out, he closed the store a few months later without selling it. This is a prominent example of an unreasonable seller.

Some brokers argue that taking any listing will give them buyer leads that they can turn to other listings. That's true but that's not a professional business model. Being true to yourself, your sellers, and your buyers is the only way to become successful. Brokers may also contend to take listings when they are overpriced knowing that they can waddle these sellers down on price over time.

You can evaluate this for yourself and make decisions on a case-by-case basis. If you think you will have a good working relationship with a seller, but the seller is pricing the business high out of greed rather than need, then you should take the listing. Just understand that you will need to make every effort to educate these sellers about pricing, time to sell, and the chances for the listing to become stale. Discuss how they can try a higher price listing for a few weeks, which should be enough time to get a sense of whether the market will bear their price. After that, they will need to reduce their price or add terms and sign an updated listing agreement. This is a reasonable request and they should come to your terms. The important take here is to stay in control of your listings. You can give sellers a little leeway, but don't let them control the sales process, you need to be the expert and in being the expert, you should educate sellers with your knowledge to make sales happen, not just to obtain listings.

There may come a time when you will have to cut sellers loose. Like my example with the liquor store seller, you too may have to decide when it's time to cut the cord. This is a personal decision that you will have to make. If you feel that you are wasting your time and you cannot convince a seller to do things your way, then you'll have to decide how long you want to continue or if it's a waste of your time. Remember that you are working on commission and you won't get paid unless the business sells. If the business is not priced right or the seller refuses to cooperate, then you won't sell the business and you won't get paid. On the flip side, I've been fired by two different sellers only to be hired back after other brokers failed to sell the businesses. I was fired because I continued to push the sellers to offer financing to buyers. Both businesses necessitated buyer financing because the sellers were leaving town and that scares buyers, but the sellers were stubborn and fired me (I was going to leave them anyway). When they re-hired me after six months or so, they both allowed me to add seller financing, they both sold at their asking prices in less than three months.

Be real with yourself, you cannot expect to take a listing on day one of your career. You'll need to work with buyers first and get to know the system and how everything works. You can see how other brokers operate and how they handle their listings and sellers. Although, it's not rocket science, you will need to have some confidence and understanding to control the conversation and communicate to sellers that you are capable of handling their transactions. Time and practice will make you confident but stick to the procedures outlined here and you will become great at it.

What types of things make businesses sellable? Location, employees, management, assets, revenue, contracts, business relationships, and the age of the business are just some of things that you should ask sellers about to find value in their businesses. If it's just a man and a truck, you may not see much value, but if the business has employees and has been in business for many years, it would be much more attractive to sell. Although you should ask about revenue, it is not the most important factor in determining if a business is sellable. You can sell businesses with sales that have suffered for years. Some buyers see opportunity in these businesses, especially if they are good at marketing and sales. The other thing to remember is that you can take a little time and do some research. Sellers aren't usually looking to exit immediately; although, they may have made up their minds to sell, they usually understand that the process will take some time. This allows you the opportunity to do some market research and to consult your broker or other agents to see if a sale is feasible.

Step-by-Step Guide

1. Start off your meetings with greetings and casual conversation. This is to see if you like the sellers and think you can work as a team together. Without a good working relationship, the business will be too difficult for you to sell.

2. Slowly turn the conversation to get the sellers talking about their businesses. Pay attention, act interested and lead with questions with the intent to obtain insight into whether the business is sellable.

3. Sometimes meetings are arranged away from businesses or after hours, so customers and employees don't find out about the sale. Either way, try to arrange meetings so you can get about 45 minutes of a seller's time without interruptions.

4. Don't accept businesses that you think you cannot sell or if you don't get along with the sellers.

5. Take your time and evaluate each business. Don't make your decision too quickly if you are unsure about the feasibility of a sale.

6. Most sellers want too much money for their business, so you will have to take some business listings even though they are initially overpriced. Make sure your sellers understand that they must lower the price or add terms after an initial listing trial period.

Get a Listing Agreement or a Retainer Agreement Before Starting Work

If you have a job without aggravations, you don't have a job. —Malcolm Forbes

Typically, brokers offer a free business valuation as a promotional tool to find business sellers. That's fine, but you should understand that sellers of companies worth listing don't expect a free valuation. What they expect is a free consultation to see if they trust you, and to make a plan of action that gets them what they need. Business owners may be curious as to their business value; however, serious sellers are more interested in whether you are the right person for the job. Focus on educating sellers about the listing and sales process and explain that the valuation is part of the listing process.

If sellers try to get you to value their businesses on the telephone, that is an indication that they may not be serious enough for you to work with. Never give a valuation over the telephone. There is too much involved to give an off-the-cuff valuation. Likewise, when I was a young attorney, clients would ask me to predict how their cases would turn out. I'd feel compelled by the pressure of the situation to give them an immediate evaluation with a probable outcome. It didn't take many times of being wrong that I learned there are too many laws, facts, and variables to consider for an off-the-cuff projection. The same thing goes for professionally evaluating businesses. Company valuations in the same industry can range from $0 up to many millions of dollars depending on many different factors. You will need to identify these factors and then apply them to the business at hand. Remember that sellers don't know anything about selling their businesses and need to be educated. Don't give off-the-cuff valuations, educate your sellers about the listing and sales process to maintain control of your listings.

Explain to sellers that you will use comparable sales to value their companies and that businesses, unlike real estate, vary greatly with revenues, earnings, locations, sizes, management, sales teams, growth rates, reputations, market shares, asset values, proprietary products, marketing processes, and in many other ways. It's irresponsible to look at a company at the first meeting and value it, in fact, it is impossible. You must consider all these variables in connection with the comparable sales listings to come up with a likely selling price based on both a cash sale and a financed sale.

Once sellers understand this point, you can explain that you will need them to sign a retainer agreement or a listing agreement with the idea of you producing a comprehensive valuation. You should also explain that you will not be listing their business until the valuation is complete and they give you written authorization to market the business at an agreed upon price. This is an important distinction to be understood about how you should operate compared to other agents. Most agents present sellers with quick valuations to entice them to sign listing agreements. You on the other hand, should educate your sellers and ask them to sign retainer agreements authorizing you to do valuations in exchange for a one-year listing. Upon signing an agreement, sellers are not committed to listing their businesses. However, they are committing to listing their businesses with you, and nobody else, if they are satisfied with their valuations and authorize you in writing to market their businesses. In essence, you are saying that you agree to value their businesses, but they cannot list it with anybody else or by themselves. This gives sellers their free valuation and it commits you to doing the work for free (or for a retainer fee) in exchange for the right to list the businesses for the next year at a price authorized by the sellers.

If you choose to use a retainer agreement rather than a listing agreement, you can do this with or without an upfront fee. Most sellers with gross sales above $2,000,000 are not opposed to giving you a retainer fee that is deductible against a final commission. The fee tends to scare away smaller businesses, so you will have to determine whether you want to try this or not. A fee of $1,000 is justifiable for small businesses but a fee of 1.5 percent of the listing price is more suitable for larger businesses. A valuation can take anywhere from 20 to 200 hours of work, so it is nice to get an upfront fee if you can to ensure you get paid for that time and effort. Nevertheless, when you start out as an agent, you should probably use a retainer agreement without an upfront fee to make things easier on yourself while you are learning.

Whether you choose to use a retainer agreement or a listing agreement, once the agreement is signed, you can present the sellers with a checklist and an outline of the process to sell their businesses. It should give them a step by step guide to the sales process along with a checklist of items that you need to do a proper valuation. The information can be extensive depending on what type of business it is, so you should start with the most important things you need and work down the list over time. Start with the financials and a listing information worksheet. These items may keep sellers busy for a week or more. Don't worry if a listing drags on for a while. Sellers are busy running their businesses and don't have a lot of time to devote to the selling process. Be patient with your sellers but keep in contact with them about your progress. The listing process may take anywhere from a week to several months to be completed properly.

Prior to sellers signing an agreement, they will need to know what your brokers fee will be. Since most business sellers have never sold a business before, they are unsure how you will earn your fee. In fact, they are usually not sure if you have fees or are paid by commission. Whether the question comes up early or late in a listing presentation, it will come up; therefore, you should be the one to bring it up. If business brokers in your area are charging a 10 percent commission upon sale, for example, you should come right out and say that your commission is 10 percent. If sellers ask if it's negotiable, say no. Price fixing is not allowed and I am not telling you to stay with 10 percent to fix commission prices. What I'm saying is if 10 percent pure commission is the custom at the time and in the area that you work, then you should probably be charging the customary rate to avoid pricing your services too cheaply or too expensive. You'll likely notice other agents starting at higher commission rates and allowing sellers to bargain them down to a lower rate. The problem with this is that anytime you get more than the customary rate, you'll have to worry about sellers finding out that you are being paid more than a standard commission, and they may get upset. This is something that you can experiment with as you get more experience, in the meantime, you should probably keep things simple and just keep your commission rate at about the customary rate in your area. You should also stay away from charging upfront fees until you become experienced. Again, since the custom is for business broker to work on a purely commission basis, it will be difficult for you to convince sellers to pay you a fee instead. For larger businesses, you can stay with the customary commission rate that you use for smaller businesses or use a graduated scale like the following: 10 percent for the first $2,000,000, 8 percent commission up to $4,000,000 and it decreases to 4 percent eventually. By the way, your listing or retainer agreement should list a minimum commission, so you will never go below that amount. This may give you a commission of more than 10 percent for anything that you sell under $150,000.

Discussing your commission with sellers is very similar to speaking with buyers for the first time. At first it will be very awkward for you to discuss and then with experience and practice the discussion will go more smoothly. New agents sometimes allow sellers to bargain them down and accept listings at lower rates than more experienced agents. There is nothing wrong with this, except the smaller pay, but there is very little that a new agent can do about it, except gain practice and experience. My advice is to not go lower than 10 percent unless you are desperate for your first listing and absolutely must give in to a seller driving a hard bargain.

Agents often overlook the fact that there are different types of listing agreements that they can use to list businesses: each will produce a different relationship between sellers and their broker but it's important to pay attention to what sellers need and use the correct agreement for each situation. Most agents focus on taking exclusive right of sale listings rather than tailoring the agreement to what is necessary or agreeable to their sellers. If you have a serious seller who has an issue with your listing agreement, then try to Taylor the listing agreement to what the seller needs. Don't come back to work empty handed, get to know and use the following information to your advantage so you don't miss out on opportunities. So, you can have sellers sign either a retainer agreement or a listing agreement to obtain an exclusive right of sale or an exclusive agency listing. Again, the difference between a retainer agreement and a listing agreement is that the retainer agreement authorizes you to do a valuation prior to listing a business, but locks in your right to list the business after the valuation is completed. A listing agreement will simply say that you are immediately obtaining the right to list a business at a certain price.

The most liberal listing is an Open listing and is often the most agreeable to sellers because it gives any broker the right to bring a buyer and get paid a commission. It is a simple agreement, usually done with a one-page form that spells out the price and terms that are acceptable to a seller. The biggest problem with open listings are that the sellers are trying to use every broker in town to bring buyers and it's very difficult to get the sellers' individual attention. It's also usually difficult to get copies of important documents which means that you almost never have the opportunity to value the listing for yourself. Sellers will provide you with their asking prices and acceptable terms. Why would a seller's agent accept this type of agreement? You often see this type of listing with gas stations, convenience stores, liquor stores, or laundromats. These types of businesses are notorious for not having documents anyway and their value is derived for the most part from their location rather than from their financial health. The important thing to remember with open listings is that you don't get paid unless you bring the buyer.

An exclusive agency agreement is given to sellers who want to retain the right to sell their businesses themselves without paying a commission. In other words, they promise to give listing brokers the exclusive right to sell and earn a commission, except for buyers that come through the sellers themselves. You can happily give this agreement to sellers who demand this because they almost never sell themselves, in fact, if they do find buyers, they will most likely turn them over to you and pay at least a partial commission because working with buyers is very time consuming, and sellers are confused about what paperwork to have signed and how to proceed to closing.

An exclusive right of sale is the exclusive right of a brokerage to sell the business, meaning the broker will get paid a commission if, and when, the business sells. The word "sells" has a specific definition in most listing agreements. It basically covers any transfer of property or right with regard to the business or the assets. It also covers the cancelation of the listing. Since businesses are easily transferred (maybe to a friend or family member) without a title company, business listings have a steep penalty for cancelation, normally the full commission.

Another type of listing, which is not really a listing at all, is referred to as a pocket listing. This means that you don't have a written agreement with a seller; however, through past dealings or word of mouth, you have knowledge that the business owner will likely sell if you present a buyer. In this case, you can use an open listing or a one-time showing agreement if you find an interested buyer. Most importantly though, you should not advertise these listings for sale without written authorization. If you have a buyer who is interested, then you can ask the seller how to proceed with the showing or gathering of financial information.

You may have heard the phrase ready, willing, and able. This is a reference to the real estate doctrine upheld in many states that protects brokers by allowing them to earn a commission if they bring a buyer ready, willing, and able to purchase a business that is for sale. Meaning that if a seller decides not to sell, then the broker still earns a commission if a buyer brings an offer equal to the terms in a business listing advertisement. Listing agreements often provide more protection than this and they allow for all parties involved to have a firm understanding of the arrangement ahead of time. Thus, in order to protect your commission and to provide your sellers with a firm understanding of the deal ahead of time, you should use a listing agreement in the strictest form that the sellers will accept.

Step-by-Step Guide

1. Most brokers offer a free valuation or consultation to find willing sellers. You should do this but make sure that you use the time to consult with sellers about the listing and sales process and educate them as to how you do valuations as part of the listing process.

2. Try to get a signed retainer prior to starting valuations. You don't want to put all that time and effort in just to have sellers go sell their business themselves or through another agent.

   - You can charge a retainer fee or not. It's your choice. You should likely wait until you are an experienced agent before trying to charge a fee.

   - Discuss the commission and be fair and honest about what you charge. Rates vary slightly but if you are high on your rate, you better be able to justify it. Sellers sometimes shop around and may have already been given a commission rate from another agent. One percent is equal to thousands of dollars and it's a very big deal to sellers if they can pay one or two percentage points less.

3. If you can't get a signed retainer or listing agreement, then you will have to decide if you still want to value the business. A full valuation report can take between 20 and 150 hours of work depending on how complex the business

is. To do anything less than a full valuation report is unprofessional. If your instinct is that you don't want the listing, then don't waste your time doing a valuation. Be upfront with the seller and maybe recommend that they try a different agent who will do the valuation for them. You can make a referral agreement with the other agent and possibly earn a fee without taking the listing.

4. Use the best listing agreement for each business. Sellers have varying needs so different agreements will work best for different sellers. Don't get it stuck in your head that you can only taking exclusive right of sale listings.

   - **Exclusive Right of Sale**—This guarantees the listing broker a commission if the broker brings a ready, willing, and able buyer, if any transfer of assets or ownership happens, or if a seller cancels the agreement. If the buyer comes through another broker, then the listing broker still gets paid a commission but chooses to share it with the other broker because of a written agreement or the association rules. If the buyer comes through the seller, then the listing broker still gets paid the full commission.

   - **Exclusive Agency**—This allows the seller to market and sell the business without paying a commission but guarantees the listing broker a commission if the broker brings a buyer.

   - **Open Listing**—This allows any broker to bring a buyer and get paid a commission. The seller retains the right to sell the business to his own buyer without paying a commission.

   - **Pocket Listing**—You don't have an agreement, but you have knowledge that the prospect might sell if you bring a buyer. Get an open listing or a one-time showing agreement prior to showing the business to ensure you get paid a commission.

5. Provide sellers with a checklist and a seller's information worksheet so they can start gathering the information you need for a valuation and for listing the business.

   - The checklist is extensive, so start with the most important items and follow up with further requests as information is needed. Don't overwhelm sellers with too much paperwork or you won't get anything back.

Gathering Information for a Valuation

If you don't know where you are going, you might wind up someplace else. —Yogi Berra

By this point, you should have a signed retainer or listing agreement. If not, you should feel confident that upon completing a valuation, you will get the listing. In order to start a valuation, you need to start educating the seller about the process and list what information that you will need. Most brokers use a checklist of items that are necessary to complete the valuation. You can do a valuation with less than all the documentation that you need to post a listing, so your initial checklist can have only the necessary items. Don't overwhelm seller prospects with too much documentation at first. Get what you need for the valuation and plan to gather more information while preparing the listing memorandum. For instance, you can do a valuation if you know what the rent amount is, but you will need a copy of the lease before you post the listing.

The absolute minimum as far as financial documents that you need for a valuation are the prior three years tax returns, a year to date profit and loss report, a current inventory report, and a list of assets. It would be nice to have a balance sheet, but most businesses can't provide one unless they have an accountant handling their financials. For larger companies that have a bookkeeper or accountant, you can use a larger list that includes things like, a breakdown of sales by month, a breakdown of sales by products and services, and a breakdown of sales by client.

Be assured that the financials only tell part of the story, for the rest of the story, you'll need information on management, employees, marketing, market share, location, and all the other details that define the business to be valued. Again, to do a valuation, you can use an outline of the information required, but before you post a listing, you will need all the details. To obtain this information, you can use a listing information worksheet form. If you allow sellers to complete it themselves, you may have to go back and interview them anyway because sellers are busy running their businesses and they are typically not detailed enough with their written answers. The form is supposed to wring out the good, the bad and the ugly in businesses so that you can analyze them from a buyer's perspective. The idea here, is to research the things that add or detract value. It's not always obvious, sometimes you have to ask a lot of questions to get sellers to really explain how their businesses can be distinguished from other similar businesses. It's not until you have all the pertinent information that you can explicitly match them up to comparable sales. It takes some experience to get good at this, but just take your time with each new valuation and go through the businesses methodically, as if you were purchasing them for yourself. The listing information worksheet form will guide you through this. Make sure you get the complete picture of each business even if you need to go back for multiple seller interviews. Most sellers have never sold a business before and they have no idea how in-depth business brokers need to be in preparation for dealing with buyers. Buyers will challenge your valuations, so you need to be very thorough.

Typically, sellers either don't realize why you need the listing documentation or are hesitant about sharing confidential information with somebody they don't know, but you can get over this by educating and familiarizing them with the sales process. On the other hand, you will find that other sellers hold back information for other reasons, namely because they are worried about their financials showing low revenue or inflated expenses. They think that if they hide this information, then they will have a better chance of selling their business. Nobody wants to pay taxes and business owners and their accountants are constantly playing a numbers game to avoid paying a lot of income tax. This is a common situation and you will be able to recast the numbers to more accurately reflect the business financials. Once you explain this to sellers, they should feel more at ease and provide you with the documents and information that you need. At the end of the day, if you can't get financials, you can't sell the business. These are actual and legitimate seller concerns, so if you prepare yourself for these conversations ahead of time, you will be able to take more listings.

Agents often ask if they can sell a business that has only been in business a year or less. The answer depends on a few factors: whether the business doing a good quantity of business, if the business just started or just purchased by the seller, if the business has a niche, its location, and why the seller is selling. The answers to these questions will help you determine if it is sellable, but it may still be difficult to value. One years' earnings or projected earnings are not enough to apply traditional formulas for valuation; therefore, you must use a little more art than science. You'll really have to dig into the industry and look at details of the business as compared to other similar businesses. Buyers will evaluate businesses looking for risk. If the business to be sold can ensure buyers that the risk is low, and the reward may be high, then it is sellable. Pricing is the main issue. In this case, there is no formula. You will need to do your research, evaluation, and let the sellers know that the price may have to be lowered substantially in case you are wrong, and buyers are not interested in the business at your asking price.

Similarly, agents ask how they should handle businesses without financials. Technically, no existing business should be without financials, but coin laundries for example, will show almost no income and almost no profit. The reason is many owners skim the cash off the books (pocket the cash without putting it on their books); hence, the term skim is used to describe the situation. Generally speaking, you shouldn't take a listing without financials because you can't sell it. But in the case of coin laundries, for example, sellers know that they can use their utility bills to prove to buyers how much business a location is doing. If their utility bill shows a certain amount of water and a certain number of kilowatts in electricity used each month, buyers can go to industry journals to see how many cycles the washers and dryers ran that month. Industry journals also indicate how long each type of machine lasts and the estimated maintenance requirements by industry standards. Coin laundries are an anomaly, conceivably gas stations and liquor stores can be sold without financials as well. With these businesses, the financial information may come from sources other than tax returns and profit and loss statements. They are difficult transactions to handle, especially for new agents. The believability of the cash is fleeting, and buyers are always wanting to see more proof. Sellers are always promising the cash is there. Even when a deal like this gets to contract, there is only an even chance that it will close. For the most part, you should leave these transactions to brokers who specialize in those industries. Your time is better spent learning to sell businesses with solid financials. Nevertheless, this will be your choice: Some brokers do very well focusing on gas stations or coin laundries, but you will have to learn those industries from a mentor or by doing the job rather than from this book.

Step-by-Step Guide

1. After you have a signed retainer agreement or listing agreement, you should obtain financial data from the seller in order to do a valuation—three years tax returns, a year-to-date profit and loss, a list of assets and inventory, and a completed listing information worksheet are the minimum requirements.

2. The information gathering phase is also the point at which you have to start educating sellers as to the sales process. You can't overload sellers with a huge list of documentation and information or they become overwhelmed and discouraged. Start with some simple requests and take your time going back and forth gathering the data that you need for the valuation. Remember that after the valuation, you will continue to gather more information that you will need for the listing.

3. Information gathering takes time and patients, but you need sellers to work with you to get your job done, so don't overwhelm them all at once. Most of them have never done this before and are relying on your guidance. Keep things easy and simple and add details slowly.

4. If a seller has an accountant, then you can request more detailed reports along with the financial documents.

5. It may take several meetings and document requests to gather everything. Take your time because sellers get frustrated when they have to stop working to do other things like call their accountant or make a list of inventories.

6. Interview sellers with a listing information worksheet form to cover over all of the aspects of their businesses. You can have sellers fill out the form ahead of time, but you will still need to ask questions and get more details about their businesses.

7. You should use checklists for yourself and for your sellers to help organize the process.

Earnings Recast

You would not believe how difficult it is to be simple and clear. People are afraid that they may be seen as a simpleton. In reality the opposite is true. —Jack Welch

Recasting is the term used for taking either profit and loss statements or tax returns and presenting a more realistic picture of the seller's profit by adjusting the financials. In other words, tax returns may take into account extra expenses like interest, depreciation, extra asset or inventory purchases, personal travel expenses, and other personal expenses of sellers. Rather than being true business expenses that should be deducted from the sellers' income, in actuality, these items are a benefit to sellers and therefore, to buyers too. Since nobody wants to pay taxes, tax returns are loaded with expenses that aren't necessarily respective of the true expenses of a business. When those items are added back to the net profit, this gives buyers a truer picture of what goes in the seller's pocket at the end of the year. For a main street or mom and pop type company this new bottom line number is referred to as seller's discretionary earnings (SDE). The bottom line, in this case, includes the owner's salary as part of the profit. For a larger company that is run by a management team, you will use Earnings, Before Interest, Taxes, Depreciation and Amortization (EBITDA) and the bottom line number does not include the owner's salary. It's normally easier to recast management run companies because main street companies often mix business and personal expenses or sometimes combine revenue with other seller-run companies. To make things worse, occasionally they don't use a bookkeeper or accountant and you will have to sort things out. Since, it could be a big liability for you if you misrepresent a seller's financials to prospective buyers, you'll need to be extremely careful under these circumstances. Perhaps you should even require sellers to hire an accountant to sort things out before your listings is posted.

In order to value businesses, you should be looking at profit rather than cash flow. Although, you may hear these terms being used interchangeably, they are different. Cash flow takes into consideration principal and interest payments on a loan, whereas, profit would only accounts for the interest expense. Cash flow is important in considering whether a business is generating enough money to meet its debt service expense, or it can be used by buyers to determine their return on investment (ROI). Nonetheless, when you value businesses, you should use either SDE or EBITDA, which is the profit after it has been recast.

Step-by-Step Guide

1. Recasting requires that you use either a business profit and loss or tax return and make adjustments to only include business revenue from the business to be valued and by removing personal expenses and other non-cash expenses.

2. EBITDA

- EBITDA is the term used to represent recast profit for companies which are operated by a management team.

- EBITDA means Earnings, Before Interest, Taxes, Depreciation, and Amortization are deducted.

- Do not add back owners' salary or benefits to the profit unless the owners are taking their salary simply as an expense to lessen their tax burden and not actually working.

- You need to leave in salaries that account for management's payroll expense because buyers will also have to pay those expenses to run the businesses.

3. SDE

- SDE is the term used to show recast profit for owner-operated companies (referred to as main street companies or mom and pop companies).

- SDE stands for Seller's Discretionary Earnings.

- SDE is calculated the same way as EBITDA, and then, you add back the owner's salary and any owner benefits and personal expenses.

- Make sure to deduct revenue from any other companies that may be incorrectly mixed in with the revenue from the company being sold.

- Be careful not to include spouse's salaries or other business owner's salaries if they are working in a necessary position at the business. For small businesses, it is assumed that one buyer will take the job of one seller and then hire employees to cover the jobs of the other sellers if there are any other sellers. Therefore, you must recast the earnings as if the buyer will have to pay new employees to do the jobs of any other sellers.

- You may have to adjust the amount of the other seller's salaries to reflect the market rate. In other words, if a second seller is taking extra profit in the form of a very large salary, then you would add back the amount of the extra salary that is above the market rate a buyer would have to pay a worker to do that job.

4. You can use a recasting worksheet included in this manual to recast companies' earnings.

- The final recast numbers are used for comparing businesses to comparable sales listings in order to come up with valuations.

How to Value Businesses for Sellers

Beware of geeks bearing formulas. —Warren Buffet

There is an old adage among business brokers, the 1-2-3 rule: Pricing a business at one times earnings will cause the business to be sold quickly, at two times earnings will take a year to sell, and at three times earnings—good luck. This illustrates the correlation between sales price and time to sell. Accordingly, as the asking price decreases, the number of available buyers (buyer pool) increases. As the buyer pool increases, so then, do the odds of a sale. You should keep this in mind and always try to increase the buyer pool for all of your listings. It's like the law of supply and demand but in the inverse. The variables available to agents which can increase the buyer pool are pricing, terms, and marketing.

Although, the 1-2-3 rule is a good ballpark when discussing valuations in a theoretical sense, as a business professional, you should use more precise and reliable methods for your clients. In fact, some businesses will sell for more than three times earnings. Some stock market companies sell for 30 times earnings or more. Even private companies can sell for 15 or 20 times earnings, especially as a result of a takeover or merger situation. There must be a good reason for this though. Investors will simply not accept the risks associated with buying small businesses if they think they will have to wait more than three years to break even. Nevertheless, in a takeover situation where a company is buying a competitor, the acquiring company may make up the difference by increasing its market share. The bottom line is that the return on investment is calculated ahead of time by buyers and the multiple of earnings they are willing to pay correlates to the projected risks and rewards.

Generally, as a small business broker, you will be dealing with companies that have net profit of at least $50,000 and maybe as high as $3,000,000. This means you will be selling businesses valued between $100,000 and $15 million. There are different methods that are used to value small businesses: a percentage of gross sales, a multiple of net income, or in the case of an asset sale, the fair market value of the assets. Small businesses by definition are generally limited to businesses with less than $20 million in revenue. Above that number, business sellers will most likely use investment bankers to get their deals done. Investment banking deals entail equity partners, multiple financing partners, accountants, attorneys, and valuation experts. These deals are not handled by business brokers and the deals are valued quite differently.

To be frank, there are about ten different known methods of business valuation computations. Some entail a complicated process and for the most part, you will need to buy a computer program to assist you with their calculations. However, as a new agent, you should focus on the most commonly used methods: the percentage of sales and multiple of net profit. These two methods are similar in that they use prior sales comparisons to show what comparable businesses have sold for based on a percentage of sales or a multiple of net profit.

If businesses in an industry have been selling for 50 percent of their average annual sales, then you would assume that a seller of the same type of business will have a comparable sales price to sales ratio. Unfortunately, every business is not average, and you will have to look at other factors to come up with a more accurate prediction of the selling price. The compared valuation price will need to be adjusted up or down based on favorable or unfavorable business conditions like location, market share, or sales growth. Thus, if a business is better than the average business in the industry, it should command a higher than average selling price.

Likewise, you can use net profit to come up with an average multiplier. The same comparable sales report can be used to obtain the average net profit multiplier in that industry and the resulting number gets multiplied by EBITDA or SDE to obtain an average valuation figure before adjustments.

You should use both methods in order to get a better picture of the health of the particular business being sold. The idea is to come up with a price range for the business being valued. Let's say a listing has higher than average revenue but lower than average profit, the high revenue indicates strength and the low margin on profit indicates weakness; still, you will still need to account for all the other factors before obtaining a value range. By gathering all the information and using a price range, you can move the valuation up or down in the price range based on all of the factors being considered. When factors indicate strength or weakness, you'll need to account for how much it will affect the price. This takes some research and analyzation of other companies. It also takes some estimation. Your initial estimation may not be perfect, and you may have to adjust the price as you learn how buyers react to your estimations. Some of the factors to consider beyond revenue and profit are earnings growth, future expected earnings, sales contracts, industry relationships, accounts receivable, inventory, intangible assets, location, lease value, market trend, industry trend, strength of employees, strength of management, condition of assets, and any other things you can think of that may add or subtract from value. The final tweak to valuations comes down to a question of how quickly an owner wants to sell. If they want to sell quickly, they can price the business aggressively, if not, they can price is high and wait for the right buyer. It is your job to come up with a valuation range and the seller's job to choose how you price it for them.

Inventory and assets are constantly an issue for brokers to deal with for valuation purposes. For the most part, inventory and assets are included in the price of businesses and not added as an extra cost. The reason being, both inventory and assets are what produce income for businesses. If you remove those things, there is usually no business left. For example, if you remove the groceries from a grocery store, there is nothing left. The same goes for a dry cleaner, if you remove the laundry machines, there is no more equipment left to do business. Buyers need to step into a business and continue using the inventory and assets to produce the same amount of sales as the sellers have. This speaks to the reason we use multiples or percentages for comparable sales: A grocery store that sells $10 million a year that is valued at 50 percent of sales is worth $5 million and a store doing $1 million is worth $500,000 but only if they are stocked with the same amount of inventory as the sellers used to gain their previous sales revenues. Some brokers will try to sell businesses with inventory listed separately. This is a problem if they are using the same multiples and adding the inventory as an extra cost to buyers. In fact, you may have sellers ask you to do that to get around paying you a commission on the inventory. The commission amount and the pricing of the business are two different things and one does not rely on the other. You'll need to stay in control of your sellers and make sure they allow you to list and sell their businesses properly.

Along the same lines, restaurants must maintain their assets to keep customers coming in. If tables and chairs get worn down, then less customer will eat at the restaurant and business goes down. Sellers simply cannot pass on the cost of capital improvements to buyers. They are selling a restaurant that is supposed to generate the same amount of business that it has over the past few years for the seller. The improvements to assets are depreciated and expensed. As in any business, seller's benefit from depreciating asset: both because they write off the depreciation each year, and because they remove depreciation as an expense when calculating SDE because it is considered a one-time expense and is removed from expenses the same way depreciation is. In essence, buyers are paying for goodwill, and goodwill is composed of future earnings. Although restaurant sellers spend a lot of money on building the kitchen, the assets are almost worthless on the open market. Restaurants derive their value from the amount of business they can generate. In this case, capital improvements are necessary to maintain the same level of business but not to bring in more business. If the assets were left to deteriorate more, business would suffer, and the valuation would drop, at the same time, by replacing these assets, business would be expected to stay the same but not increase. Sellers can add back the capital improvement expense minus any depreciation taken in that year, but they cannot simply add the amount of the improvement to the price of the business.

Let's take a look at an example of two restaurants: They both have SDE earnings of $150,000 a year and are valued at 1.5 times earnings or $225,000. One restaurant has assets with a value of $50,000 and the other has assets with a value of $150,000. Now, let's look at why the restaurant with the higher asset values is only valued at $225,000; maybe the original asset cost was $300,000 and the assets deteriorated, so the restaurant is doing less business than it did in the past; maybe the restaurant lost its manager; or maybe it's in a poor location. It could be for any of those reasons or several other reasons, but it doesn't matter what the reason is. Unless the buyer is buying the business as an asset sale, the buyer is buying the goodwill (a multiple of SDE) and both businesses throw off the same SDE each year. What good is it to pay more for assets that generate the same return as cheaper assets?

Alternatively, let's say a bus company just paid $500,000 for a new bus the week before your valuation and the reason for the purchase was the company needed an extra bus to bid on a contract. In this case, the asset is not currently being used to generate the income that you are using to value the business, therefore, it's not included in the sales price and the company can charge extra money for the bus. The same can be said for a grocery store that gets a delivery just before the closing of a sale. Any amount of inventory above the average amount of stock should be an extra cost to a buyer. The idea is that we are basing the sales price on inventory and assets that are necessary to maintain the same sales figures for the buyer as the seller.

Try not to let buyers and sellers get involved in valuations, especially when it comes to asset and inventory prices. Sellers tend to overvalue their assets and inventory and buyers tend to discount the value. Obtaining the actual fair market value of inventory and equipment is nearly impossible, for the most part, there is no active market to sell these assets, so, there is no way to put a precise value on them. Agents routinely use sellers' numbers as a starting price for asset values, but it's a good idea to ask sellers for a range rather than a specific value to give yourself a little wiggle room. Inventory is easier to deal with than equipment; however, even inventory can vary in price on a daily basis. Just imagine dealing with inventory that is months or years old. To make matters worse, most small businesses don't track inventory well.

Pricing businesses can be complex, especially when it's a larger company with large assets and different revenue sources, perhaps even proprietary products or licenses are involved. In this case, you should be aware that there are business valuation experts who can handle valuations. A valuation can cost a few hundred dollars or thousands of dollars depending on the time involved. There are also business valuation guides and websites that track business sold listings to help you when doing valuations. It's probably not a good idea to use a service since you are supposed to be the expert. I'd imagine that most sellers would object to hiring the third-party company and perhaps lose confidence in you if you recommend that they do. Your best bet is to ask your broker for assistance. Although business valuations can become complex, that just means that they will be more time consuming to list. It may take several weeks to a month before you can gather all the information and decipher it.

Another important aspect to be considered when doing valuations is to distinguish the target buyers for each business. Different buyers will pay different amounts for the same business. A strategic or competitor buyer is looking to buy the accounts or the location from a competitor and will likely pay the lowest amount of any buyer. Their motivation is to take over more market share in their industry. They are basically looking for asset sales. The most common type of buyer that small business brokers work with is the income buyer. These buyers are looking to buy a job and work in the businesses. They are generally looking to leverage their money and buy a business with the largest net profit that they can afford. If they pay cash for a business, then they expect a deep discount. If they are able to finance a business, then they are willing to pay an average price or a bit higher than average based on the amount of financing available to them. Their main concern is to maximize the yearly take-home pay from the business. A loan payment doesn't usually have a large effect on the take home pay, so they are willing to pay more for a business as long as they can finance the extra price difference. The last type of buyer is the equity fund. This is normally a group of investors, but sometimes only one or two wealthy investors. They are looking for a return on their income and they don't want to work in the business. Their criteria usually include businesses with management in place, and net profit (EBITDA) over $500,000. It is common for investors to pay multiples of seven times EBITDA or more. Thus, you need to be aware of your target buyer and price the business accordingly.

Step-by-Step Guide

1. Generally speaking, the "1-2-3 Rule" works for small retail companies. Agents should notice the correlation between the decreasing price and the shorter time it takes to sell a business. This is because the buyer pool increases as the price decreases, and the more buyer you have, the greater the chance you have of selling.

2. If a business is priced too high, buyers will not inquire because they know it is overpriced and they think the seller is playing games. When the price is lowered, the same buyers will still not inquire about the business because in their minds, the seller is not somebody they want to deal with. The term used to describe this is, the listing is stale. Try to avoid your listings becoming stale.

   - Procedure for valuing a business using a multiple of cash flow or a percentage of gross sales:

     - Search for comparable sales listings (comps) with a service provider or a business MLS.

     - Adjust the comps for location and amount of gross sales by removing any comps that don't match the business being sold.

     - Location is normally not too important but try to stay in the same state. If there are not enough comparable sales in the state, then look nationally. Businesses in California have generally sold for higher multiples over the years, but most other states have similar multiples for valuation purposes.

- Larger businesses in the same industry may have different ratios to use for valuation purposes because different buyers will pay different multiples. For example, an equity fund will pay more than an income investor for the same business, but equity funds only want larger businesses.; therefore, once a business is big enough to attract an equity fund, the ratios will change. Be sure to adjust your comparable sales listings so you are using the best matches to the business being sold.

3. Check the comparable sales report to see if the ratios include assets and inventory. You need to make sure you are comparing apples to apples. Some services will separate assets from goodwill. If that is the case, you will have to recalculate the ratios after adding the assets back to the prices.

- The exception to this is if a business was sold with real estate. In that case, you will not include the real estate in the selling price. In fact, if your comps include assets and inventory in the sold prices, you will have to remove the value of the real estate and readjust those sold prices.

4. Now, calculate the following two ratios from the comparable sales report: business sold price divided by the yearly gross sales, and business sold price divided by net profit. Do this for each business on the list.

5. Average all of the ratio numbers. Once for sold price to gross sales, and once for sold price to net profit. These two average figures are your average multipliers.

6. You may also use a business broker reference guide to obtain these average multipliers. There are commercial guide books, software, or websites that can provide you this information without you having to do the calculations.

7. Recast the financial statements for your business being compared. Recasting means to create a profit and loss statement and remove the following expenses: the owner's salary, depreciation, amortization, interest, any personal expenses of the seller's that are not legitimate business expenses. This will give you SDE. If you want EBITDA, just remove interest, taxes, depreciation, and amortization.

- Recasting may also entail removing revenue from the gross sales if it is from another company or product line that is not part of the business being sold.

- Use financials from the prior three years if possible to come up with the average gross sales and average EBITDA or SDE. You will not get a good valuation number from looking only at the most recent year or the current projected year. You must use an average of the last two or three years if possible.

8. Multiply the average multiplier, from Step 7 above, for gross sales by the gross sales from the business being sold. Then multiply the average multiplier for the net profit with the net profit (SDE or EBITDA) of the business being sold, to get the two resulting valuations for the business being valued.

   • The numbers will be slightly different but shouldn't be too far apart because businesses in the same industries should have similar margins.

   • The resulting valuation numbers are your valuation range based on average sold prices.

9. The final step is to adjust the valuation range up or down based on the strength of the business being sold. This is more of an art than a science, which is a skill that you will develop over time with experience. If the business is strong, adjust the range prices up a certain percentage. If the business looks weak compared to your comparable sales, then adjust the price range down a certain percentage. It's difficult for you to know what percentage to use at first because you won't have a feel for how each strength or weakness affects the final selling price. Get the help of your broker or an experienced agent if you are having trouble at this.

Try to Get Your Sellers to Give Terms

Take a method and try it. If it fails, admit it frankly and try another. But above all, try something.
—Franklin Roosevelt

Terms is the word used to describe seller financing. Seller financing is when sellers hold a note for part of the purchase price. Sometimes a note is secured by a lien on assets. This is advantageous to buyers because they can leverage their money without having to get a bank loan, and it provides buyers with some security because sellers are accepting some of the risk of the business going forward. Sellers are generally okay with offering a small loan because, in most cases, they sell their businesses quicker and for more money than they would without offering terms. There is also a tax advantage to sellers that comes from receiving their money over time rather than in the same tax year. Offering terms is especially important if you cannot get a business approved for a SBA loan.

Even when a business can receive SBA loan approval, you can still have trouble finding qualified buyers since the SBA has stringent requirements when it comes to buyer's past loan or payment history. Since this can limit the buyer pool, you'll need to use seller financing to compensate for the buyer qualification issue. Buyers want to leverage their money and look for businesses that offer financing.

Financing, and seller financing even more so, weigh heavily on a business sales price. We live in the age of credit. Everybody expects to finance everything. So, when buyers have $200,000 to spend purchasing a business, they expect to leverage that money and purchase a business worth double or triple that amount. For the most part, these buyers won't even enter search criteria for businesses worth less than $300,000. This means that if you have a business selling for $200,000, you won't see the buyers with $200,000 because they will be looking at larger businesses. Most of your buyers will have $70,000 to $100,000 and will expect to finance the balance of the $200,000 business with their money as a down payment. Hence, the greater the amount of financing you can provide for them, whether it be through sellers or through SBA loans, the larger the buyer pool you will attract for that business.

Cash buyers on the other hand, will expect a steep discount, somewhere in the neighborhood of 30 percent to 50 percent. Therefore, you really have two different prices for each business, the financed price and the cash price which will is deeply discounted. It's not that you will advertise two prices, but you should expect that buyers with cash are not willing to pay as much as other buyers.

Sellers are typically afraid to finance buyers because they immediately think about how difficult it could be to collect if a buyer defaults. This is a legitimate concern and you will need to deal with it each time to have a chance of selling their businesses. Remember that buyers don't usually look for businesses that they can pay cash for. They are looking to leverage their money, or if they are willing to pay cash, they will expect a steep discount on the price. This means that in order for you to sell businesses efficiently, you need to convince your sellers to finance some of the cost of the purchase price.

The main benefit to sellers offering terms to buyer is that they sell their businesses in a shorter period and for a higher price than sellers that don't offer terms. Most of the comparable sales listings will be for businesses that sold with some sort of financing, therefore, the average multipliers are based on businesses being sold with financing rather than cash sales. To sell a business for cash, sellers will simply have to discount the price.

Other benefits to sellers include earning interest on the money they finance at a good rate. The exact rate of interest is negotiable, but customarily it is equal to what lenders are charging on commercial loans: Today's rate is about 6 percent but in recent years it has been as high as 8 percent. Sellers should also pay a lower tax rate because they are receiving the money over time rather than reporting the money as a large income in one tax year.

It's also important to discuss how the lending process works and their remedies in the case of a default. First of all, the sellers will have the final say as to whether they finance a buyer or not. You will have all the buyers apply for financing just like if they were going to a bank for a loan. You will pull their credit reports. If anything doesn't look right, you can ask them for a co-signer or a lien on their personal assets. The point is that you should explain to sellers that they are not just giving credit to anybody off the street. All the buyers will be screened and approved based on the seller's consent. And in the rare case that a buyer defaults, the seller can take back the assets and restart the business. This is much easier to do with retail locations, but I have seen some service companies take back their businesses. The sellers can then build business back up and re-sell the business to another buyer. Technically, sellers can do this without an attorney, but it would be prudent to get the assistance of an attorney and an accountant when taking back the assets of a business.

How much seller financing is enough? Somewhere around 70 percent of all business sales have some amount of seller loan attached to the deal. Of the 70 percent of financed deals, more than half have seller financing of at least 25 percent and some as high as 60 percent. If the business has enough lien-able assets, and the buyer has good credit, then sellers are likely to be more willing to provide the financing. The other thing you can remind your sellers of is that if you get a buyer with good credit and that buyer is willing to put down a large amount of money, in other words, a few hundred thousand dollars, there is very little chance that the buyer will walk away from that down payment money, and as long as the business continues to operate, sellers will get paid, or they can repossess the assets, build it back up, and sell it again.

Step-by-Step Guide

1. Sellers who don't offer terms get 70 percent of their asking price on average and some receive much lower. That means that the cash discount for business purchases is about 30 percent.

2. Sellers who give terms get 86 percent of their selling price on average, they sell their businesses faster, and sell their businesses more often.

    -   Sellers holding notes will receive an additional six percent or so each year on the balance (depending on the negotiated interest rate).

    -   There are usually tax advantages to taking income over time rather than in a lump sum.

    -   There are methods of using assets to secure seller financing, such as, motor vehicle liens, UCCs, and security agreements. It's even possible for buyers to pledge mortgages on their residential homes to secure seller financing for deals.

3. If you have listings that are not selling because the prices are too high, ask your sellers to give terms and change the listings to show that it can be purchased with a down payment rather than the full cash price. Sometimes, this is more desirable for sellers than lowering the asking price. Buyers tend to negotiate the down payment rather than the final price. This means that the sellers can get their price, but they will have to allow for some terms.

How to Handle Skim (Cash)

Don't find fault, find remedy. —Henry Ford

Some business owners who receive a lot of cash revenue don't report all or some of the cash on their tax returns. Shocking! The money is referred to as skim because it is skimmed off the top line of the books by the sellers. The issue for sellers is that when they sell, they want to have their cake and eat it too. In other words, sellers don't want to report the cash revenue to avoid the taxes associated with it, but they expect to have buyers pay for the value of the revenue when purchasing their businesses. Except for certain businesses, like laundromats, gas stations, convenience stores, liquor stores, and sometimes bars and restaurants, buyers won't give any value to cash revenue. The difference with these other businesses is that they are location sensitive for the most part. In other words, most of their value can be derived from their location and their rent payment. If their rent is market value or better and their location is known for the right type of traffic, then buyers will acknowledge value without absolute proof of the revenues.

Believe it or not, most owners keep a second set of books to track cash. Some do this electronically but some use old fashioned paper records. They do this for the same reason they keep the first set of books, to track sales and margins. Owners need to know their revenue and expenses to track changes and make to advertising, orders, payroll, and other expenses. Owners simply need to monitor their businesses whether they are skimming cash or not.

The issue for buyers then becomes the believability of the second set of books. With most businesses, they don't give any credibility to the cash; however, as mentioned above, there are some businesses that can be sold based on the skimmed cash revenue. Besides the fact that they are location sensitive businesses, the industries also allow sellers to prove their cash by using methods other than tax returns. Bars, for example, can show that a certain number of bottles were purchased from their distributor each month, and knowing their drink prices, it will represent a certain amount of income in sales for the purchased liquor. Similarly, a coin laundry can show a water bill which represents a certain number of gallons used each month and can be used to calculate how many times the machines were cycled; hence, how many washes were purchased by customers. As noted above, these industries are location sensitive and they will stay in business or go out of business based almost entirely on their location and the rent they pay. A good location with a good rent payment will attract a lot of buyers for and the sellers will be able to use their skim for valuation purposes. Again, it's only in these few above-listed niche industries where buyers will give cash any credence for valuation purposes.

With businesses in any other industries, besides the ones known for owners skimming cash, buyers will not rely on incidental proof of revenue. The risk of being deceived is great and buyers are weary of this. On the flip side, sellers don't want to miss out on any possible added value to their sales price. They know the skimmed revenue is there and want to get paid for its value. It's easy to understand both positions, however; it usually winds up being a balancing act for agents trying to put deals like these together. One of the best ways to handle this situation is with an earn-out arrangement, where sellers get some of the purchase price upfront and earn the rest in monthly, quarterly, or yearly payments based on meeting sales figures using a trackable index. You can't use revenue because it will be skimmed, so you have to find another way to track sales. Sellers are not always as amenable as buyers to this type of arrangement, so to entice the sellers, buyers can offer to pay higher earn-out rates or bonuses based on sales that come in higher than expected. Other than an earn-out arrangement, buyers may sometimes be amenable to a long due diligence period where they have an observation period, meaning they can sit and watch a business for a month and count customer purchases. This may work for some sellers but not for sellers who have proprietary processes, or client or vendor relationships that they want to protect.

As far as legal consequences pose for you selling cash businesses with suspect tax returns; as far as I know, there is no duty to report suspect businesses or owners to the IRS. Although you may believe the tax returns are suspect, in actuality, there is usually very little proof. And, unless you are conspiring to defraud the IRS, there is probably no legal duty to report these businesses to the IRS. It's the same situation for state sales tax and payroll taxes. As long as you are not involved in any fraud, there is not likely any legal duty to report a possible violation. The issue with sales tax is that sellers are probably not reporting the correct amount of revenue to the state, and therefore, not paying sales tax on that revenue (if applicable). Along the same lines, payroll tax may be due if employees are receiving cash off the books. That said, most state tax departments are much more likely to come after business owners or to make arrests than the IRS if they do suspect wrongdoing with payroll taxes.

Then again, becoming liable for your clients becomes a trickier situation to figure out. Whether you can be forced to share in the past due tax burden by an implicated buyer or seller is a conversation that industry experts have been having for years. The best advice is to avoid this situation completely and keep all conspicuous cash revenue out of your listings. Let buyers and sellers speak about cash with each other and let the written record reveal nothing about unreported cash revenue or off-the-books employees. Also, make sure that sellers sign a written approval of the financial figures used in their listings to avoid any fraud, misconception, or conspiracy accusations, and make sure the numbers on the tax returns match your financial spreadsheets used for listings. You want to be like Colonel Klink from Hogan's Heroes, "I know nothinnnnng."

You may be wondering about how you will handle a restaurant or coin laundry that shows very little revenue if you find one to sell. My advice is to keep cash revenue out of your listings. Many agents choose to show the skimmed cash or off-the-book employees because they are afraid of not selling the business without this information in their listings. Ultimately, it's your decision to risk going to jail, being sued, or possibly sharing in your client's tax burden. At the end of the day, the businesses we are talking about, all generate revenue based on their location. A good location will attract buyers and then you can lead them to a discussion with your sellers about the cash situation.

Step-by-Step Guide

1. Skim or unreported cash is illegal and can get unsuspecting agents into legal trouble.

2. You will need to make your own policy decision on how to handle skim.

3. Some agents choose to show the skim and have sellers sign an approval of the financial figures shown as, "owner to prove" or something to that effect to indicate that the numbers do not come from a financial report, but they are numbers received by the agent from the seller.

   - This is still risky, and I would recommend using the real figures obtained from the tax returns.

   - If the business is location sensitive, then it will attract buyers and you can let buyers and sellers discuss the cash situation in person.

   - If the business is not location sensitive, then sellers will not likely receive full value for the cash revenue in their sales price, so there is absolutely no reason to put it in the listing. Sellers can sometimes take advantage of an earn-out arrangement, but they still won't get the full value of the cash revenue.

4. Remind buyers that nobody wants to pay too much in taxes, so the tax returns are the worst-case scenario for business financials. On the other hand, skim is not completely believable either, and it represents the best-case scenario for business financials.

5. Laundromats, gas stations, convenience stores, liquor stores, bars, and restaurants are notorious for unreported cash sales. To help prove the cash figures, bars can use bottle purchases to prove their numbers, coin laundries can use utility bills, and sometimes convenience stores will allow a buyer to stake out the business for a week or two and count customer sales.

   - Although you shouldn't post the added cash revenue in your listings, you should consider the revenue for valuation purposes.

- Try not to include skim in any other listing valuation, other than for laundromats, gas stations, convenience stores, liquor stores, bars, and restaurants. Since, it's not common in other industries, it's very difficult to convince buyers to look at secondary evidence to prove the cash revenue. A second set of books is simply not believable. Remember, the reasons that you can sell businesses that are skimming are because it is common in these niche industries, so buyer expect it, the secondary evidence is conclusive, and because the locations of these businesses hold a high value with buyers.

6. If you can't get buyers and sellers to agree on how to value a company, see if they will agree on a higher price based on an earn-out arrangement where sellers get a down payment and then a percentage of sales monthly or quarterly based on hitting sales figures. Sometimes, you can offer a buyer a 50 percent partnership until the final payment is made and then the other 50 percent gets transferred. In any case, sellers will probably require buyers to put all of the unpaid money into escrow to be drawn upon as goals are met.

- With earn-out arrangements, you cannot use revenue as the target index because the revenue will be skimmed and is not trackable. You'll need to use a trackable index. Purchases usually represent the best way to do this. As businesses turn over product, they need to purchase more. This gives buyers and sellers a direct correlation to sales.

Leave the Door Open for a Price Reduction

Begin with the end in mind. —Norman Brinker

Business valuations change with market and industry trends. Evidence of this can be seen with the price of businesses on the stock market, which change momentarily. You should to be aware of this with regard to small business listings as well; if there aren't any buyers interested in a listing because it's overpriced, you need to lower that price quickly to avoid a stale listing. A helpful hint is that you should always try to price listings no higher than 20 percent above the expected sales price and less on larger listings. With stocks, as the bidding prices fall, so do the asking prices. Similarly, your asking price will be higher than the expected offer price, but those numbers can't be too far apart, or you won't make the deal happen.

To curtail stale listings and poor buyer responses, you should have a conversation with your sellers ahead of time, especially sellers who demand unreasonable asking prices. You might explain to a seller that buyers are not going to overpay for his business. When buyers look at small businesses they see risk. To limit that risk, they try to invest as little as possible. We can overcome this by providing a seller with value. Value means that we have priced the business appropriately and are not trying to take advantage of a buyer. If a buyer thinks a seller is being unfair with pricing, then the buyer won't make an offer on the business. We need buyers to take us seriously and make offers in order to sell the business; therefore, we need to have the business priced appropriately.

If you must, you may allow an insistent seller to start out with a high listing price under the condition that you monitor the buyer response in the first few weeks and reset the listing price to a reasonable level if the response is poor. Failure to have this conversation prior to listing businesses at unreasonable prices, will make it very uncomfortable for you to try to get sellers to lower their prices after their listings are posted. In fact, most agents who fail to have the conversation before, hardly ever win the argument for a lower price later and their listings rarely sell. You need buyers in order to sell listings, if you don't get buyers, then the businesses are priced out of the market and won't sell. This is the salient reason that 78 percent of the listings on the market never sell.

Step-by-Step Guide

1. No amount of marketing will make up for an overpriced listing. You need buyers to sell listings and buyers won't make offers on excessively overpriced listings.

2. You should make every effort to price listings no more than 20 percent over their expected selling price, and then prep the sellers for the possibility of having to lower the asking price by a certain amount after a month or so if you get disappointing buyer feedback.

   - If sellers are not prepped ahead of time for the possibility of a price reduction, then they will be upset and opposed to it. They think the reason for the business not selling or showing well is that you are not doing your job. They may even see you as an adversary rather than an advisor and it will be difficult to get them to agree to a price reduction.

   - Have the conversation about pricing with your sellers ahead of time and prepare them to lower the asking price within a few weeks of the original listing.

   - If sellers are not in agreement with your pricing plan, then you may not want to waste of your time with their listings.

Get Your Listings Prequalified for SBA Financing

If you do a little more than your competition, you'll stand head and shoulders above them.
—Ed Moore

The US Small Business Administration has a program that backs a portion of loans that are made to business owners for startup, for building up existing businesses, or to business buyers for business acquisitions. Business buyers can be approved for up to 85 percent financing but may also be approved for further loans for extra working capital. Although a buyer would still be required to come up with a down payment of 15-25 percent, technically, this can amount to 100 percent financing for the cost of the business in some cases. You should work closely with an SBA loan representative or a commercial loan broker who can keep you apprised of your options for each business deal.

The process starts with a very informal application for the listing business; where, a lender provides pre-qualification based on the last three years tax returns and very little else. Pre-qualification significantly increases the chances of selling businesses and may also increase their selling prices. SBA financing attracts a lot of buyers to listings because it allows buyers to leverage their money at a very low interest rate over a ten-year term or longer if the purchase includes real estate.

The SBA and some lenders may not allow financing on certain types of businesses, like, lending businesses and casinos. Furthermore, you will find that schools, gas stations, restaurants and bars are difficult to finance because some banks either have stringent cash flow guidelines for them or decide to avoid them altogether.

Once a business is prequalified for an SBA loan, you must have interested buyers make a formal application for the loan. The loans are known for being paperwork intensive but can usually be done in a matter of a few days. The formal approval of the loan takes a few weeks but is usually done within 30 days. Once a buyer is approved, funding the loan can take another 45 to 60 days to fund an SBA loan. So, the entire process takes about 60 to 90 days from start to funding at the closing.

Step-by-Step Guide

1. Contact some local banks who advertise that they provide SBA loans and meet with the representatives to get their lending criteria. Then contact some private lenders rather than banks that issue SBA loans. Since these lenders are privately owned and fund their own loans, they have different criteria than most banks. You will find that some lenders will be willing to fund gas stations, while banks are usually not. You can use this to make a network of lenders and you can have pre-qualification approvals from multiple lenders for each listing. It's okay to use a commercial loan broker as well, they will scout the lenders for you and assist the buyers with the paperwork. Normally, commercial brokers charge buyers an extra fee for their services. The other problem with brokers is that they may have too many deals going on and tend to focus their time on the easy deals and if you run into trouble on a deal, they may not be as helpful as you need them to be.

2. Email the last three year's business tax returns and a year-to-date profit and loss with the asking price and any other information that you have about the business to the bank representatives or commercial lending broker for SBA lender pre-qualification.

3. The representatives should email or call you back within 48 hours with SBA pre-qualification or with a reason that the business doesn't qualify. Remember to use your network. Some banks will say no to some businesses while other banks or lenders will approve the loans.

Create Offering Memorandums for Listings

If I believe in something, I sell it and sell it hard. –Estee Lauder

An Offering Memorandum or Confidential Business Review (memo or CBR) is a memorandum about a business summarizing all of its characteristics: clientele, advertising, management, market share, products and services, industry trends, etc. A well written memorandum can help sell a business faster than without one or with a poorly written one. In order to generate good offering memorandums, you must take the time to do a thorough interview with your sellers and gather all of the details about each business.

When buyers come to you through advertisements about businesses for sale, the first thing the buyers ask is for you to tell them more about the opportunity. Without writing that information down, you won't remember every aspect about every business that you sell, so to be responsible and professional, you must write that information written down for future use by buyers. The other reason that you need to make good memorandums is because you can walk buyers through the story of the business, tell them about the benefits, show them the opportunities, list comparable sales information, and show how you justify the asking price. You can't do all of that in a conversation or it would take a few days to complete. Sometimes buyers want to share the information with partners, attorneys, or accountants. They need the information in writing to do this and the memo is the vehicle for it.

Surprisingly, too many agents don't use memorandums and of the agents that do, many of them put together poorly constructed ones. Agents don't like putting them together because it takes time and effort, so often times they use basic information or copy information from the business website, which is basically, useless. Other agents use information that is simply incorrect. Remember, that buyers sometimes send these to their attorneys and accountants. Misrepresenting a business in writing is more than just sloppy, it can be a liability for you. Image what buyers think when they search for businesses and see so many poorly written memorandums: They must think that all business brokers are scammers. Hence, it's important that you use memorandums to stand out in the crowd and look professional among the den of thieves. It's also important that you put the time into each so that they are done thoroughly and correctly. If you do this, buyers will be much more likely to believe your review and valuation of the business and they will be ready to deal with you because you come off as a professional.

Step-by-Step Guide

1. Offering memorandums can be long or short depending on the complexity of the business deal.

2. Do your research and create thorough and professional memorandums for all of your businesses.

   - Buyers will notice the difference between your memorandums and most of the rest of the brokers. This will make your listings more believable and sellable.

   - It may take several weeks or months to gather all of the relevant information and for you to learn the seller's business, but until you do this, you won't have a sellable business or a complete and thorough offering memo.

Advertise Listings

We need not apologize for being zealous advocates for our clients. —Michael Richardson

Listings should be broadcast throughout all available channels in order to attract the largest possible buyer pool. Simply listing a business in a MLS alone is a common mistake made by new agents. Generally, businesses generate fewer leads than real estate listings and therefore, need a more comprehensive marketing campaign. Advertising listings has the added benefit of attracting buyers who may buy a different listing even if they don't buy the advertised listing.

The sites listed below are the most widely used for advertising businesses, but you should also search the internet for business listing sites in your local area to look for new sites worth trying. Most new sites start with a free or low-cost initial "test" rate to allow you to try their site. There are new sites being created every year and you should keep an eye out for them. Another good source for advertising can be a local newspaper with a business opportunities classifieds section. The response rate is well worth the small price of placing a classified ad. When placing ads in the newspaper or on Craigslist.com, you should note that generic ads don't work as well as ads for specific listings. Buyers won't respond to an ad that says call me if you want to buy a business, but they will call for ads that say I have laundromats for sale in the local area. Take a look at the two advertisements below and see how the second one is more likely to generate a response:

- Businesses for Sale: All types, Low Down Payment, call John Broker (561)-000-0000
- Gas Station for sale on corner in downtown Ft. Lauderdale $150,000 Down and Financing Available. This one won't last! Call Broker Bill Directly at (561)-000-0000

Step-by-Step Guide

1. The following is a list of websites that you should absolutely use to advertise business listings. You can use other sites, but these are some of the most used sites in the industry.

   - Your local business MLS
   - www.Bizbuysell.com
   - www.Bizquest.com
   - www.businessesforsale.com for international buyers.
   - www.Bizbuysell.com for businesses that include real estate, like gas stations.

2. You can also place for sale ads in your local newspaper classifieds if they have a business opportunity section.

3. For franchises, there are sites that specialize in advertising listings for franchise brokers. These sites are very costly, so you will want to make sure that you are specializing in franchise business sales before you get a membership.

4. For companies that are run by a management team and have a net profit of more than $500,000, there are specialty websites such as www.Axial.com that will attract the attention of mezzanine funds, hedge funds, and wealthy investors.

Stay in Contact with Sellers

You have to do what you have to do, to do what you want to do. —Kurt Wulf

After listing their businesses, sellers will be anxious to hear from you. If they don't, they will assume the worst: either that you are not doing any work for them or the listings did not produce any buyers. You will need to stay in contact with your sellers every few weeks and give them feedback. During every listing period, you will need to screen and prequalify buyers, sometimes as many as thirty or more buyers. Sellers need to know that part of your job is to screen buyers to keep them from wasting their time on unqualified buyers or "tire kickers." Keep the line of communication open with sellers so they don't get discouraged with you. Let them know that you are dealing with buyers but that you haven't been able to find a good qualified candidate among the ones so far. Remaining in contact with sellers has the added benefit of keeping their enthusiasm level up and they tend to be more helpful when they are enthused rather than disappointed.

The entire sales process can last a year or so and during that time, you will need to update financials and other key business indicators to keep your listings current. In fact, occasionally, you may have sellers go out of business during the listing period. Sometimes this can't be avoided, but I think that lowering the price and getting something is better than just closing the doors and walking away. To avoid this situation, it's important to stay in contact with sellers. Sellers are busy with their day to day jobs associated with running their businesses and they don't always think that they can help their listing broker by working with them. Therefore, it's your job to stay in touch with sellers and to create the team atmosphere. By staying in touch, creating a team atmosphere, and keeping an eye out for sales trends, you will do a much better job and your sellers will be confident with your representation.

Step-by-Step Guide

1. You should schedule seller status calls on a calendar program to every two weeks to ask how their businesses are doing. Ask if they gained any contracts, bought any assets, started a new advertising campaign, etc.

2. The financials can be updated monthly but should at least be updated quarterly.

3. Be proactive, stay in touch with sellers, teach them how you will need to work together to sell their company. They will need your feedback, and you will need them to communicate how their business is doing going forward.

Easy vs. Difficult Businesses to Sell

Real life doesn't travel in a perfect straight line; it doesn't necessarily have the "all lived happily ever after" bit. You have to work on where you're going.
—Chris Kyle

This topic speaks to supply and demand: There is a different demand for gas station listings than there is for golf courses for example. If you were to list a golf course, it might take two years to sell because there is generally a shortage of buyers for businesses like that. However, if you list a gas station, buyers will call daily about the listing. Therefore, it's much more desirable to list gas stations than golf courses because gas stations will sell quickly due to the high demand. It will also generate a lot of buyer leads that can be turned to other gas station listings.

If you decide to try to sell a golf course type listing, then you can't simply list it and wait for the phone to ring. The best course of action is to call all the other golf course owners in the area and ask if they want to expand their operation and purchase the listing. Amazingly, you will find that this type of campaign usually generates other listings, as some of the owners you call may want to sell their golf courses or other businesses they own. Anyway, you will be networking, which is integral with deal making. Golf course owners can also refer you to industry associations and other contacts that might be of help. Listings with limited buyer pools may take two years to sell, but networking is the only way to sell them.

A golf course is an extreme example, but there are plenty of other business categories that are not very easy to sell, and some examples are listed below. The point is that with some listings, like a gas station, you can post them online and wait for the phone to ring; but with others, like golf courses, you will need to be proactive and create your own deals through networking. Business owners are generally happy to speak with you and give you advice. Developing a network of business owners has the dual purpose of assisting with the sale of the listing you are working on and creating a system of people to refer listings to you in the future. Agents who understand this and act on all of their listings will sell many more businesses through their network as time goes by than agents who only list and wait for the telephone to ring.

Step-by-Step Guide

1. It can take a few years to sell some businesses, but these are anomalies, and most should sell between four and nine months.

2. Easy businesses to sell are generally restaurants, gas stations, dry cleaners, coin laundries, franchises, liquor stores, c-stores, and the like, because they have a big buyer pool to draw from. They are location sensitive and can be run by somebody without a higher education or business experience, so they attract a lot of buyers.

3. Difficult businesses are golf courses, schools, professional offices, internet websites, general contractors, and any businesses that needs a particular skill or expertise to run.

    •   For difficult listings, you should start networking by calling similar companies to see if they want to buy the listing. If not, the listing may sit on the market without attracting buyers.

    •   Ask the buyers you call to refer you to other possible buyers and industry associations or trade magazines.

    •   The bottom line is that you have to actively sell a difficult business in order to have a chance at finding a buyer: Networking with other brokers, calling prospective buyers, contacting industry associations, and advertising in industry journals are ways of increasing attention to these listing.

Prequalify Buyers Prior to Meetings or Showings

A fool with a plan is better than genius without a plan. —Boone Pickens

As a listing agent, you will need to make sure that selling agents bring you prequal-ified buyers before you introduce them to your sellers. When sellers are informed about a potential buyer that is requesting a meeting or a showing, they get very excited and will take time out of their busy day to meet with the buyer. If a buyer is not actually qualified to purchase the business, the sellers get very upset. Some sellers may even switch brokers after too many such occurrences.

To avoid this, you need to make sure buyers are qualified both financially and for experience prior to meetings with sellers. If you are unable to qualify a buyer but feel that the buyer is still a good candidate, then make sure sellers understand the issue surrounding the buyer. If the buyer is short on cash, then explain to the seller that the buyer qualifies in all other ways but is short on cash. Sellers can make the decision whether to meet or not as long as they understand ahead of time that the buyer needs seller financing. If buyers aren't qualified with a license or a compatible background, make sure sellers understand this before you set up meetings and give sellers the choice to meet with the buyers. You shouldn't auto-matically turn away unqualified buyers. Sometimes deals can still be made, but it's important to advise sellers of the situation and give them the choice to deal with buyers or not.

Try to team up with sellers and treat their businesses as if you are also an owner. Don't be so focused on making deals that you forget to do your due diligence as an agent. Take the time to interview buyers or their agents and get to know who you are dealing with. Be careful and methodical in order to be professional and successful as an agent.

Step-by-Step Guide

1. Prequalify buyers financially prior to arranging meetings with sellers: Make sure buyers have the funds to purchase the business being sought. You should have the buyers fill out a buyer profile form or if a buyer has a business broker agent, you should have the agent prequalify their buyer and send a written profile form or financial statement for your review.

    *   If buyers are short on funds, then send them to a bank or loan broker and ask for proof of the results.

    *   Alternatively, advise sellers that a buyer only has a certain amount of money available to purchase their business and let them decide to finance

the buyer's deficit or not.

- Often time, sellers will finance a buyer if they like the buyer. This is despite the fact that the same sellers will tell you that they won't finance anybody.

2. Make sure buyers are qualified to purchase a business with respect to experience, certification, visa requirements, etc.

- Have buyers fill out a business buyer's profile and financial worksheet prior to introducing buyers to sellers.

- Putting unscreened buyers in front of sellers can be disastrous and may result in sellers cancelling your listings.

Agency Representation and Negotiations

Trust but verify. —Ronald Reagan

There are different types of agency and representation for brokers and they vary with state law. There is the single agency or dual agency representation. In Florida and some other states, the dual agency is referred to as a transaction broker. Under a single agency agreement, you are representing either the buyer or the seller but not both. As a transaction broker or under dual agency representation, you are providing limited representation to both parties, and should remain neutral. A transaction broker is a deal maker who needs to maintain a fair, honest, and neutral position with respect to buyers and sellers. Neutrality means that you are not allowed to let buyers know that the sellers will accept less or vice versa. This is a tightrope to walk but has its benefits. The main benefit is that you can streamline transactions by assisting both sides with limited representation.

Since it's generally accepted that business listing prices are negotiable, it is a bit of a quandary to remain compliant while dealing with negotiations. Although you are not allowed to let a buyer know that your sellers will accept less than the offer prices or negotiate terms that are better than the listed terms, you are allowed do this with your seller's permission. The same goes for a buyer's agent. If both agents come to the table with ballpark figures, then you will have a starting point for negotiations. Sometimes price is not the bigger issue. If there is a bigger issue, then find out what the other side is looking for. It's important that you don't hurt your seller's position by giving up the bottom line or negotiating against your client's interest. Once both agents are armed with the understanding of what the other side needs, it's easier to create deals that everybody can live with. If you are the only agent on a deal, then find out what the buyer needs to feel comfortable with the deal. Do this when the sellers are not present, so buyers can speak freely. Then, make sure that you have permission to go back to the seller with some of that information. You can't go back and forth with confidential information, but you can go back and forth with information that the other side allows you to share.

Negotiating deals whether as a single agent representing one party or a transaction agent remaining neutral requires experience and knowledge. There are many courses on how to negotiate deals by using certain questions or certain body language. You can study these courses and read about the psychology behind deal making, but the bottom line is that you always need to understand what the other side needs before you can negotiate a successful deal. In fact, the best way to get that information is to ask. Just keep saying, "Tell me what you need?" If a buyer needs time, then ask the seller what it would take to buy the buyer the time needed. If a seller needs more money, then ask the buyer how we can structure the deal to get the seller the extra money he needs, maybe the buyer will hire the seller back to do contract work. You can't make deals by bringing sellers low offers and having sellers counter with high demands. Find out what each side needs to make the deal happen and then try to fulfill those needs.

Put all offers in writing with either a letter of intent or an asset purchase agreement. An LOI is not a firm commitment, but a way of bringing deals to the table just prior to being finalized with purchase agreements. The reasons that deals should be in writing are two-fold: one, because, buyers and sellers tend to make faint promises with spoken words and change their minds easily; and two, because it is not as emotional as negotiating verbally and people will act more reasonably. If an offer is done with an LOI, then the stated issues need to be resolved within days and you should move to a signed purchase agreement shortly thereafter. If not, you should continue to market the business to other buyers. Remember, for a written contract of sale to be valid, it needs a promise (buyer's offer in writing to seller), acceptance (seller signs the agreement and delivers it back to the buyer), and some consideration (down payment). If an LOI does not turn into a purchase agreement shortly after it is accepted, then continue to pursue other buyers.

It can be acceptable to start negotiating verbally but you should try to keep that between the agents: meaning that the agents are relaying information to each other from their respective clients. Never allow buyers and sellers to negotiate with each other verbally. The more aggressive side will win the negotiation and the other side won't feel good about the deal. It will be a very difficult deal to close in the end. Putting offers and counter-offers in writing avoids misrepresentations, misunderstandings, and changes in mind. More specifically, it helps you keep control over the negotiations by documenting the understanding of all parties.

Step-by-Step Guide

1. Ask selling agents and buyers to bring you their offer price and terms to try to establish a base for opening negotiations.

   - Remember that you can only disclose confidential information such as the acceptable price with your client's permission.

- You also have to understand your agency relationship and the duties associated with that towards your client.

- As a dual agent, you should remain neutral. You should try to understand what each side is looking for, so you can try to establish a happy medium and obtain a successful deal. You can only relay prices, terms, and any other confidential information with clients' permissions.

- If you are representing a seller as a single agent, then your job is to advocate for your client. In this case, you are not looking for a happy medium, but the highest price and best terms that will get the deal done for your client. There is a subtle difference, but you should be aware of your duties to your client and any other parties to a transaction.

2. Try to get offers in writing in the form of asset purchase agreements. Also, remember that a contract is not valid without consideration and there must be a down payment.

3. Put offers in writing to avoid faint promises and to keep buyers and sellers from negotiating from an emotional standpoint.

4. Keep in mind that letters of intent and proposals are generally not enforceable.

- Investors, rather than first time buyers, may prefer to use a LOI instead of a purchase agreement in order to see if the seller is willing to negotiate on a low offer.

- The purpose of the LOI is to show a seller that a buyer is serious and would like to make a firm offer, but there is a sticking point that needs to be worked out prior to making a firm commitment.

Make Counter-Offers Quickly

When the cup is full, carry it carefully. —Andy McCarthy

Be sure to move deals ahead quickly in the early stages of negotiation and contract signing. Buyers easily change their minds after thinking about their commitment: this is called buyer's remorse, where buyers tend to get cold feet and back out of deals soon after making offers. You should try to get purchase agreements signed the same day to avoid buyers thinking about things overnight over and becoming remorseful about the deal.

The idea is not to lock buyers into deals that they don't want, but since there are so many variables to think about in consideration of buying businesses, given time, buyers' minds drift to the negative aspects and they get worried. Sure, they can cancel a contract soon after signing it, but once the contract is signed, they are in a positive state of mind and are able to see themselves working in the business as the new owner and they feel good about it. It's generally the time between making the offer and waiting for the seller's response that is susceptible to the remorseful thoughts; basically, when they feel they can still back out.

Step-by-Step Guide

1. Buyers can get buyer's remorse and pull their offers. Keep negotiations moving along and lock deals in with signed agreements in order to avoid this.

2. Make counter-offers the same day if possible. Stress the importance of responding quickly to your sellers.

3. Once buyers have signed, they tend to think positively about the business deal and the remorseful thoughts are not as prevalent.

Due Diligence

Sometimes you can observe a lot just watching. —Yogi Berra

The due diligence period is generally a short period of time (five to ten days) after the purchase agreement is executed and prior to closing when buyers have the opportunity to look over the business operations, contracts, and financials to see if they match the advertised listing. The length of the due diligence period is subject to negotiation. A normal review of financials and documents can be done in a matter of hours or a few days, that is not to say that buyers can find and hire an accountant in that time. Therefore, the period is normally a week or two. It's not uncommon for buyers to request longer, but for sellers, it's better to give buyers the minimum that they need to complete the process. If buyers are not satisfied with the results of due diligence, they can cancel the agreement and receive their deposit back, so the shorter the period for sellers, the better. Essentially, this gives buyers a full out under the agreement for any reason during the due diligence period. Typically, you will have longer periods for due diligence with cash businesses, where buyers want to take the opportunity to watch the businesses and count cash over a month period. Some contracts say that due diligence starts automatically, and some say that buyers must request items from sellers to start the process. You will need to read each contract in order to find out how to start the due diligence process and to find the length of time allowed for buyers.

Some buyers will use an attorney or an accountant to assist them with a financial review of the documents during due diligence. If a buyer needs an attorney or an accountant, look for a deal friendly one. Deal friendly professionals should become part of your business broker network. Attorneys and accountants who practice in the field of business sales will be knowledgeable and helpful to buyers, whereas, those who do not regularly practice in this field will tend to cause issues and delay and ruin your deals. There are a few ways this will happen, the first is when an unaccustomed professional tells their client that they are paying too much and to renegotiate the deal. The second is when they make overly burdensome requests for information. The reason they do these things is not perfectly clear, but it can be assumed that their lack of knowledge in the industry leads them to be overly cautious out of fear of liability.

If due diligence does not go well, meaning, that the review turned up things that a buyer was unaware of or disliked, the buyer will need to make a request to cancel the purchase agreement and get the down payment back. This request is normally made in writing, but you will need to read the agreement to determine just how and when the request is made and served on the other parties. Buyers who retain an attorney can use their attorney to make the request.

If due diligence goes well and the time expires without the buyer canceling the agreement, the down payment is locked in and the parties should proceed to closing. At this point any down payment becomes locked with respect to the due diligence clause and the buyer cannot receive the money back if cancellation is sent from this point forward. Of course, buyers may have the right to cancel the agreement under other clauses such as a financing contingency clause. If due diligence ends early because a buyer finishes early, then a buyer can sign a waiver or a certification that due diligence is over, and the parties can proceed to closing.

Step-by-Step Guide

1. You should read each purchase agreement to determine how the due diligence period starts and how long it lasts.

   - Commonly with contracts, the word days means to count every day; however, some contracts specifically say to count business days, which exclude Saturday, Sundays, and Federal Holidays. Each state has its own laws and customs, so you will have to become familiar with the laws in the state that you are working in. It is generally accepted that the first day of due diligence is not counted as a day because it is not a full day. So, if due diligence starts on January 1 and goes for ten days, then due diligence would end on January 11. Again, state laws will dictate if due diligence ends a day or two later if January 11 falls on a weekend. Laws also diverge as to the exact time that due diligence ends: at the close of business, the end of the day, or before business on the next day.

2. Your duties during due diligence include obtaining documents for buyers, answering questions or relaying the information to get answers to questions, and arranging any in-person meetings or reviews scheduled at the business

location.

3. Due diligence ends automatically on a scheduled date or it can end earlier with the written consent of a willing buyer.

What to do if Due Diligence Doesn't go Well

The single and most dangerous word to be spoken in business is no. The second most dangerous word is yes. It is possible to avoid saying either. —Lois Wyse

If you are working professionally by doing your research and creating comprehensive business memorandums, then due diligence should go well because there are no unknown elements to surprise buyers, and your deals can move forward towards closing. Unfortunately, some buyers use due diligence as an opportunity to put pressure on sellers to reduce the price. This is not to say that you couldn't have missed something during your analysis of a business. There is always a slight risk of that happening and if it does you will have to bring the parties back to the negotiating table and rework the deal to suit the new circumstances. If on the other hand, you suspect that a buyer is trying to pressure your seller, you'll need to have a strategy discussion with your seller. The best strategy under these circumstances is to walk away from the negotiations. This is only if you suspect that the buyer is being unfair. Let me be clear, you'll want to have your sellers renegotiate a deal if a buyer is being fair, but not if a buyer is being unfair.

You might think that walking away from deals will cause too many deals to break up, but the opposite is true. Most buyers will not walk away, they are simply trying desperately for a last-minute discount in price. The ones that do walk away initially will often return in a week or so to try to put the deal back together. More often than not, when deals don't go through, it's because sellers get upset with the buyers' poor form and refuse to deal with those buyers any further. The takeaway here is to always create comprehensive and informative memorandums that include accurate financials so there are no surprises during due diligence, and your sellers shouldn't have to renegotiate their contract prices.

At worst case scenario, the buyer will cancel the contract. As long as the cancellation is in accordance with the purchase agreement, the escrow agent will return the buyers deposit and you can put the business back on the market. If you think the cancelation is not in accordance with the purchase agreement because it is too late or because of any other reason, the seller can enter a dispute with the escrow agent claiming a right to all or some of the escrow deposit. It's usually a good idea to advise your sellers to have an attorney handle this for them. At any rate, this is not something that you should handle for sellers because it involves legal representation.

Step-by-Step Guide

1. If you missed an issue in your analysis of a business and it comes up during due diligence, then you can have the buyer and seller renegotiate the deal in light of the new circumstances.

2. If you suspect that the buyer is trying to pressure the seller to lower the sales price, then the best strategy is not to renegotiate the contract. Most of the time buyers will acquiesce in the end.

After Due Diligence, Before Closing

The beginning is the most important part of the work. —Plato

Bank Financing

The business will not close until the bank is ready, so this is a priority.

SBA financing is something that needs to be started ahead of due diligence but continues until closing; however, there is very little to do unless you are also working as the buyer's agent. For an SBA loan, the lending bank will have some financial document requests for sellers. Once the underwriting is finished the bank may also do a review of the assets and ask for titles or registrations if applicable. Most of the bank request involve sending them paperwork that your sellers already have on hand. If there is seller financing involved, then you will need to relay the amount and terms to the closing attorney who will handle the closing paperwork.

With regards to real estate, If the real estate is being purchased by a buyer as well as the business, then there may be a second contract of sale defining the real estate only. The contract will likely state that it is contingent upon and subject to the closing of the business contract. There should be a clause in each contract making them contingent on each other to close simultaneously. Accordingly, there may be a lending bank to deal with. Buyers can use SBA loans to purchase the real estate or they can use a commercial loan. Either way, the buyer's representative will handle most of the liaising with the lending bank.

Assignment of the Lease

Some landlords need a month notice, so start the process with due diligence.

If the real estate is being leased by the seller and the buyer plans to keep the business at the same location, then the seller's agent will need to assist the buyer or the buyer's agent with an assignment of lease or a new lease from the landlord. This is something that can be started soon after the purchase agreement is signed but is not finalized until closing. The reason that it is started early in the process is that some landlords can take weeks to get the paperwork done. They may have a lengthy approval process or a slow management agent or attorney. Also, since commercial leases are not standard like most residential leases, you should read your seller's lease and become familiar with the terms and conditions. This will be helpful with assisting with the transfer of the lease to a buyer. Although some leases contain some highly restrictive clauses and hefty fees with respect to transfer, you should not be afraid to contact landlords or management agents and try to renegotiate a better deal. Commercial landlords are businessmen who simply want to keep their units occupied and earning rent; they will sometimes renegotiate the terms of an existing lease to keep the unit occupied by a strong tenant.

Inventory

Be prepared to have an inventory company take an accounting one day prior to closing.

If a business contains trackable inventory, then the inventory will need to be accounted for on the day of or the day before closing. Normally this is done by a third-party inventory company, but buyers and sellers can agree to use the sellers existing inventory program or to do an accounting themselves. Companies that maintain small amounts of inventory used for servicing their customers will not require an inventory company; however, buyers may want to account for the inventory if the value is substantial. This is either done through invoice tracking and by a walkthrough. It is possible to do the inventory accounting after closing if the parties agree. Normally, the closing attorney would hold money in escrow to handle any adjustments that need to be made to the price once the accounting is finished.

Also, make sure to tell your sellers that unless it is otherwise agreed to by the buyer in advance, they shouldn't sell everything in the store without restocking it. The buyer will need the inventory to continue running the business and if the seller goes and sells more inventory than was promised in the contract, then the purchase price will be reduced by that amount at closing and the buyer will be upset. If there is extra inventory at closing, then the buyer will purchase it from the seller at closing.

Assets: Be prepared to transfer assets with titles at closing

As far as assets go, any assets that have titles or registrations such as automobiles or boats will have to be transferred at closing. The closing agent should handle the transfer paperwork and the person in title will have to sign the transfer paperwork. The condition of the assets can be a point of contention, but for the most part, buyers are buying the goodwill and don't focus on the condition of the assets at closing. Besides, the most expensive assets normally have insurance on them or a service contract, so it's not much of a concern. Occasionally, you can have a buyer or seller who is confused about an included or excluded asset. In this case, the purchase agreement will control which assets are included and which are excluded from the sale. The most common scenario is to have a buyer think they are getting the sellers personal vehicle with the business. Sometimes, sellers will sell their personal vehicle with the business if it is used daily to conduct business, like, a contractor's pickup truck. Part of your job is to separate personal assets and business assets and make this part of your memorandum report and eventually part of the purchase agreement so there is no confusion at the closing.

Business Licensing: Start this process with due diligence—sometimes it's quick and simple, but sometimes it's not

Business licensing is a very important issue and the process should be started soon after contract signing. Many buyers are first time buyers and require assistance with setting up their new business. For the most part, the listing agent is not involved unless the buyer is unrepresented and then the listing agent will need to provide some assistance. Normally, buyers will have their accountant or attorney set up their new company, but they won't help them apply for the necessary business licenses. Licensing requirements vary with business type and business location. Look at it this way, if a seller has a license or permit, then the buyer will need the same thing. Occasionally, this can be done by submitting simple paperwork to the state or the controlling municipality, but other licenses will require qualifications or inspections. If the business sells food or beverages, then most likely it will require many different premises inspections: health, fire, zoning, etc. That is not to mention the necessary licenses for alcohol and tobacco, which may be transferable but also may have lengthy and expensive procedures. These are things that you can learn by asking your sellers or by calling the agencies responsible for issuing the licenses. After the first time you handle each transfer or application, you should establish a procedure for the next time to be prepared. The problem with me teaching you how to assist buyers with obtaining business licenses is that there are so many possibilities and the laws and requirements vary with each location. They not only vary from state to state or county to county, but they even vary between local towns and villages. The good news is that the municipalities are normally very helpful when you call and ask questions. Remember, if the seller or the existing business has a license or permit, then the buyer and the new business will need the same thing.

If a business owner is required to have an occupational license, then this also may be a lengthy process requiring qualification and examinations. It is not uncommon for sellers to offer to qualify a business with their occupational license for a fee while buyers obtain their license. An agreement to do this is not always easy to negotiate and sellers are not always willing to qualify every buyer. This is something that is usually negotiable but needs to be discussed with sellers prior to being offered to buyers. The way I approach the situation is to educate these sellers prior to listing the business that since the business has a required occupational license attached to it, this limits the buyer pool to buyers who have that license. To attract more buyers, sellers can offer to qualify a buyer during the term it takes to obtain that license or to find another qualifier. Another qualifier may be a person that the buyer hires to run the business like a chief pilot for an airline. Not every business license qualifier has to be an owner.

Merchant Account

Start this a week or two prior to closing.

Sometimes overlooked by new agents is the transfer of a merchant account. This is not applicable to all businesses, but very important for retail businesses. Most of the time, it is beneficial for buyers to transfer the seller's existing merchant account to their new business name and bank account because new merchant accounts are more restrictive and have lower monthly sales limits. In either case, buyers will need to apply and set up a merchant account prior to closing because their business will not be able to accept credit cards until the setup is finalized. Closing attorneys are aware of the possibility of overlap or delays and they will sometimes hold escrow money to reimburse parties for transactions that are mis-applied by the old or new merchant accounts.

What Happens if I'm Not Ready to Close?

We don't live in a perfect world and not everything that you try to do before closing will work out exactly as shown above. In many cases, you can still get to closing if the parties agree to the closing agent holding some money in escrow while the parties work out the details of any unfinished items. In fact, most purchase agreements provide for an escrow holdback for a month or so, to handle any issues that come up after closing or to adjust discrepancies that come up between the two parties. Furthermore, there may be other unforeseen issues that some to light prior to closing. It's impossible to imagine all the possible scenarios, but things happen, and you'll just have to deal with them as best you can or let the deal break up and put the business back on the market. If you are doing things right, there will be few and far between deals that break up at any stage.

Step-by-Step Guide

1. Financing is generally handled directly by buyers and their lenders, but lenders will have some paperwork requests for the sellers as well. The requests should be straightforward and easy to handle. Buyers should apply for financing immediately, even before starting due diligence, because the process can take 30 to 60 days or more.

2. Work with the buyer's agent and the landlord to obtain an assignment of lease or a new lease. You can start this process prior to the end of due diligence if you like.

3. Make arrangements to provide a final inventory accounting at closing.

4. Make sure that you send any asset title or registrations to the closing agent, so they can be transferred at the closing.

5. Some businesses have very few licensing requirements, but others can be very stringent and time consuming. Try to work out the licensing with buyers so they don't have a lapse between buying the business and the day they can start operating.

6. Make sure the buyer applies for merchant account and the proper transfer of accounts is made on the day of closing.

7. Follow up with all parties, their attorneys, and the closing agent until the closing to help work out any issues.

Non-Compete and Buyer Training

Give, but give until it hurts. —Mother Teresa

As part of the purchase price of the businesses, sellers will agree not to compete with buyers within a certain area and over a certain period. In other words, if a seller sells a grocery store in a town, the buyer will have the seller sign an agreement promising not to open another grocery store in that town and perhaps in the next town over. The specifics of the agreement are up for negotiation and will vary in detail depending on the business involved. The agreements are subject to much litigation, so they should be handled by an attorney. Some agreements have been struck down because they were too restrictive and prevented sellers from earning a living after the sale of the business. In any case, for small businesses, the agreements will normally restrict a seller from entering the same or very similar business within ten or twenty miles from the old business and for a period of three to five years.

Also included in the purchase price of the business is training for the buyers. With small businesses, this training is either provided by the seller or by a manager and can last between one and four weeks. If buyers need further training than what was agreed to in the purchase agreement, sellers can choose to provide it at an extra cost to buyers. In fact, occasionally, buyers will hire sellers to work either on a salary basis or a contracted basis as needed for six months or longer just to make sure business continues as usual. This is especially helpful to buyers when they are worried about business contracts or relationships.

Step-by-Step Guide

1. You should assist buyers and sellers in negotiating the basics of the non-compete

agreement for the purchase agreement, but the specific language is written in a formal agreement that is signed at closing. Your sellers may want to have an attorney review or negotiate the drafting of the agreement for them because they are occasionally the source of litigation.

2. Sellers will normally train their buyers to operate the business after the closing for an agreed amount of time. If more time is needed, then the sellers can agree to continue the training for payment. The training is usually agreed to in the purchase agreement and included in the purchase price.

3. It is not uncommon for buyers to hire sellers to continue to work for the company on a salary or as a consultant. This should be negotiated before the purchase agreement is signed or at least prior to closing. This agreement is separate from the free training offered by sellers as included in the purchase price.

CHAPTER 42

Marketing

Chance favors the prepared mind. —Louis Pasteur

Accelerated Learning Tip

Most agents look to their brokers to provide leads. Don't count on making a living if this is your preferred source of leads. You will need to obtain your own leads. The only way to do this is by working your career like a business of its own. You will need a marketing budget, the same as all other businesses have. Find some initial operating cash before you start and continue to set aside a portion of each commission to put towards marketing. Marketing is not free and without a budget to spend on marketing, you won't generate enough sales to stay in business.

Real-Life Experience

I've tried to market business sales by mailing postcards and letters, used telemarketer calling campaigns, hanging door cards, in-person visits, educational seminars, website SEO, and Google AdWords. I haven't had the guts to try television or radio, but in my experience, the only thing that truly works is consistency. All of the marketing mediums have some affect but until business owners are ready to sell, they won't make contact. I've seen this recently when a business owner brought a letter to our initial meeting that I mailed to his business five years prior. You can choose all or some of the methods mentioned, but whatever methods you choose, do them consistently for the best results.

How Well Can You Do?

Selling businesses is a numbers game. Marketing helps create a pipeline of leads that become customers and eventually closed deals; more leads equals more closings. There is no shortage of buyers or sellers in this industry. One study showed that an average of 20 percent of all businesses in the U.S. are for sale at any one time, or about 5,000,000 businesses for sale. Another study showed, as compared to real estate the ratio of business brokers to businesses is about 1/1500 and the ratio of real estate sales persons to homes is about 1/500.

How many listings does an agent need to be successful? The average successful business agent has 13 listings and sells about 50 percent of that inventory each year. That said, an agent with that many listings will also be busy servicing buyers. If an agent closes the same number of buyers as sellers each year, then that would be 12 closings on average each year. In 2017 the average selling price for a business in Florida was about $325,000. Most successful agents have listings much higher than the averages. With nine closings an agent would have earned about $195,000. Again, these are average numbers based on the average successful agent and you will strive for obtaining a much higher than average success because you've read this book and have knowledge that most of the other agents don't start out with.

How many buyers should you have in order to be successful? Statistics show that it takes 34 telephone calls from buyers, 13 in person visits with buyers, or 3 showings in order to close one deal. It appears that the more familiar you get with buyers, the higher the chances of closing deals. Let's assume that each listing attracts on average two inquiries a week for each of the 13 listings; which is 26 inquiries on 13 listings each week. Statistically, this should give the agent at least one closed deal per month.

On average, new agents need a few months of working buyers or sellers before they typically start closing deals, but remember it's all about the numbers, if you work harder to fill the pipeline sooner, things will happen sooner.

The other issue is that it's very difficult to work both buyers and sellers. It's best to choose to work with one or the other. That's not to say that if you choose to work with sellers that you can't work the buyer for those listings, it's just difficult to show those buyers other listings. Buyer will distract you from your sellers and vice versa. Therefore, working buyers only will allow you to show buyers any listings in the MLS. You can become good at marketing buyers and working them until they close. On the other hand, you can choose to market sellers, become good at selling businesses and only work the buyers that come to see your listings. If you try to market and work both buyers and sellers, you won't have enough time to handle everything and easily become frustrated because your deals will suffer. For the most part, the most successful agents market and work sellers and buyers who are interested in those listings only.

Sell Existing Listings

Believe you will be successful and you will. —Dale Carnegie

One way to get started is to pick a favorite business for sale on your MLS and get to know competitors in the same industry. Maybe it's pizza restaurants. Contact other restaurants letting them know you have a similar business for sale and asking if they'd be interested in expanding with an acquisition. They may pass on the opportunity, but statistically, this is a proven technique for finding new listings. You may find out the owner is interested in selling and gain a future client.

By the way, by doing this, you are normally not violating any MLS rules. The rules usually say that an agent cannot advertise another agent's listing without permission, but it would defeat the purpose of an MLS to say that an agent cannot sell another agent's listing. Just be sure to have buyers sign NDAs prior to releasing any confidential information about the listings.

Advertise House Listings

I want to do it because I want to do it. —Amelia Earhart

Most brokers and their agents will freely give new agents permission to go out and advertise some of their listings. These are known as house listings. If the brokerage doesn't have a policy on it, then the agent should ask for permission from fellow agents. We've all been the new guy or gal in the office and know how tough it is to get the ball rolling. Most agents are willing to help, especially in business brokerage. Residential real estate is another story where they may actually eat you alive for asking.

Assuming that you do get permission to advertise a listing or two, put them on craigslist under business offered by dealer or put an ad in the local newspaper classified ads under business opportunities on weekends. The ads should do a good job at generating buyer leads.

Get Listings!

Idleness and pride tax with a heavier hand than kings and parliaments. —Benjamin Franklin

Get Listings, get listings, and get listings. Did I say get listings? Successful agents get listings. It can be intimidating to jump in the deep water when you are learning, but the best way to learn is to jump right in. You've finished my book and have all of the knowledge at hand to do the job. If you follow the steps as outlined, you should be able to find a local business broker to work for, pick up your first client, and get your first closing. And, I'm confident that before you know it, you'll be earning a six-figure salary as a business broker. As a new agent, you need to start doing their job in order to learn it. Typically, you will make some mistakes, but then you can do a self-evaluation to figure out what to do differently the next time. After three or four listings, your confidence level comes right up and then you will truly be a business broker. Remember that every listing will bring you many buyers. Shoot for one listing each month and then go for one each week.

Postcards

Never look backwards or you will fall down the stairs. —Rudyard Kipling

Postcard mailing campaigns have never been very successful for me; I assume it's because employees and secretaries throw them away with the junk mail before business owners get to see them. The way to use postcards is to put them on business doors at night. Often, it's the owners who take the cards off the doors while opening the business before the employees come in. The card can simply say, "Thinking of selling? Call me for a free business valuation." The cards can be taped, or rubber banded to doors in retail shopping centers. They aren't usually very big businesses, but they are simple businesses, easy to sell, and they attract a lot of buyers.

Use Letters

Ain't nuthin in life is dead solid perfect. —Dan Jenkins

You can easily download mailing lists and create a letter for mailing to business owners. Nowadays, many public libraries allow access to business databases for free, so agents rarely have to buy the lists anymore. Some agents choose to buy the lists because they can buy targeted lists, or they come with emails, so they can do a simultaneous email campaign with the mailing. In any case, you can get lists very cheaply or for free. To gain access to a free database, consult your public library online sources to see if they are available. As far as paid databases go, DatabaseUSA. com and Hoovers.com are some of the most widely used companies.

Letters have a different affect then postcards: Letters tend to make it to business owners, whereas post cards may not because secretaries tend to throw them away with the junk mail. In my experience, targeted letters work better than generic letters. In other words, if you mail letters to grocery store owners saying that you have buyers for grocery stores, this letter would get a better response than a letter to all of the businesses in an area that says, "we sell businesses." A sample letter is included in the forms section of this book.

Web Page or Website

Luck is the residue of design. —Branch Rickey

Although the internet isn't likely the best bang for the buck as far as the cost per lead goes for sellers, it is the easiest and cheapest way to find buyers. All you have to do is make a website and pay Google AdWords or a marketing company to generate traffic to your site. Websites can attract buyers and sellers. To attract sellers, you'll need an informational website. A site that attracts sellers can be costly to create and maintain.

The cost of SEO initially can be in the thousands and ongoing can be thousands of dollars more a year. Using Google AdWords as well or in addition to SEO would add thousands of more dollars to your budget. These things all work, it's just that they are very expensive, especially when you are new and just starting out.

Perhaps the cheapest way to maintain a website that attracts sellers is to create a blog. You can either create and add the content yourself or you can hire writers for this. Each blog article can cost you from $25 to $100 to make which then gets posted to your site to attract sellers. It's difficult for me to tell you what the best way is to do things here, because I use all of the techniques and can't quite figure which are best. They all seem to work to some extent.

Alternatively, to attract buyers, you will need a MLS feed with listings that buyers can search on your site. A buyer's site will require less content and SEO because buyers are only looking for businesses for sale rather than for information like sellers. Therefore, your upfront cost can be cheaper, and your ongoing cost is cheaper. The MLS feed will come through a business broker association MLS, like IBBA or the Business Brokers of Florida. The cost of the feed is likely to be less than $100 a month. The bigger cost here comes from either using a SEO company or Google AdWords to attract buyers to the site. In my estimation, you shouldn't have to spend more than $3,000 in Google AdWords a year to attract enough buyers to keep one agent constantly busy with buyer leads. As I mentioned, buyers are easier and cheaper to find online than sellers are. Also, make sure to use the website address on your email signature and on any letters and cards that you send so prospects know that businesses can be searched, and you can be contacted through your site.

Network

Isn't it common sense, that if you are going to learn something, you go to the masters?
—Tony Bennett

This is face to face marketing. You need to keep saying, "Hi, I sell businesses..." which will generate conversations and eventually somebody will send you a referral. Business groups are a great place to network with other business owners. Some examples of business groups to join are BNI, Rotary, and your local Chamber of Commerce.

Networking is the most important aspect that you should focus on as a new agent. Simply, start telling everybody that you sell businesses for a living. When you do that, you will develop some very good contacts and pick up some clients. One of the best marketing tools that you have is your mouth (and business cards).

When you tell people that you sell businesses for a living, you will start getting referrals. Everybody will be interested in what you do and want to tell you about somebody who needs your services. It really is that easy. There are not many people in our profession and most people you speak with do not even know it's a profession.

BECOME A BUSINESS BROKER

You have just finished this book on how to become a business broker: Now, go make some business cards, join a good brokerage, set some goals and start your career. Finding a business brokerage is not difficult. Start by researching business brokers in your area and then call some of the agents and ask how they like working there. Some brokerages offer training programs but from what I've heard, you'll have ten times the knowledge after reading this book then you'll gain from a one- or two-day course with a broker. Either way, in a few years, you will be glad you took the leap of faith and made the transition to become a business broker. The transition will not be terribly simple, but it also won't be too difficult and can be attained by almost anybody. It's the school of hard knocks but it won't take too long before you feel comfortable, and it's fun and exciting. I hope that you enjoyed the book and I'd appreciate the opportunity to respond to any comments or questions regarding the book or about your new career.

My email is william@floridabizmls.com.

Glossary

- **Adjusted Net Income also referred to as "Owner's Benefit" or "Net to Owner" or "SDE"**

  A seller's total earnings (or profit). Adjusted net income is calculated by taking sales and adjusting for all expenses, and then adding back the owner's salary and all items of a personal nature that were expensed. This number is calculated by business brokers as a way to show purchasers the amount of money that the seller takes in as profit each year. The number is generally higher than what shows on a seller's financial statements as profit or net income. The formula is Adjusted Net = Sales – Expenses (excluding interest, taxes, depreciation and amortization) – Personal Expenses.

- **Asset**

  All real, personal, or intellectual property owned by the business that has a financial value.

- **Balance Sheet**

  Financial statement listing a business's assets, liabilities, and equity.

- **Cash Flow**

  An accounting representation showing how much of the cash generated by a business remains after all expenses and principal repayment on financing are paid.

- **Cost of Goods Sold (COGS)**

  The cost to a business of making the products it sells. The cost of goods sold includes parts and labor expenses, but does not include shipping, advertising, or other indirect costs.

- **Depreciation**

  Spreading out of the original cost over the estimated life of the assets such as plant and equipment. Depreciation reduces taxable income.

- **EBDITA**

  Calculated by looking at earnings before the deduction of interest expenses, taxes, depreciation, and amortization. The formula is: EBITDA = Sales – Expenses (excluding interest, taxes, depreciation and amortization)

- **Franchise**

  A corporation that sells the right to use its name and business model to other companies. It is a technique that is used to raise capital and expand a business. The other companies that purchase the rights are referred to as franchisees.

- **Goodwill**
  An intangible asset that arises as a result of the acquisition of one company by another for a premium. The value of a company's brand name, customer base, customer relations, vendor or client contracts, client lists, good employee relations and any patents or proprietary technology represent goodwill. Goodwill is considered an intangible asset because it is not a physical asset like buildings or equipment.

- **Gross Profit**
  A company's gross sales minus its cost of goods sold. Gross profit is a company's residual profit after selling a product or service and deducting the cost associated with its production and sale.

- **Gross Sales (Revenue)**
  A measure of overall sales that isn't adjusted for customer discounts or returns, calculated simply by adding all sales invoices.

- **Income Statement or P&L**
  A financial statement that measures a business's financial performance over a specific accounting period. Financial performance is assessed by giving a summary of how the business incurs its revenues and expenses through both operating and non-operating activities. It also shows the net profit or loss incurred over a specific accounting period, typically over a fiscal quarter or year.

- **Intangible Asset**
  An asset that is not physical in nature. Corporate intellectual property (items such as patents, trademarks, copyrights, business methodologies), goodwill and brand recognition are all common intangible assets.

- **LOI (Letter of Intent) also referred to as a Proposal**
  A letter of intent (LOI), simply stated it is a short document that details a purchaser's intention to buy a business or commercial property and outlines a variety of details or conditions that are involved in the potential purchase. Typically, the LOI is a non-binding agreement.

- **Margin**
  In a general business context, the difference between a product's (or service's) selling price and the cost of production.

- **Net Income**
  A company's total earnings (or profit). Net income is calculated by taking revenues and adjusting for all expenses. This number is found on a company's income statement and is an important measure of how profitable a company is over a period of time.

- **Purchase Agreement**

  The agreement that serves as the contract of sale for a business. It can either be in the form of an asset purchase agreement or a stock purchase agreement.

- **Profit Margin**

  A ratio of profitability calculated as net income divided by revenues, or net profits divided by sales. It measures how much out of every dollar of sales a company actually keeps in earnings. Profit margin is very useful when comparing companies in similar industries. A higher profit margin indicates a more profitable company that has better control over its costs compared to its competitors. Profit margin is displayed as a percentage; a 30 percent profit margin, for example, means the company has a net income of $0.30 for each dollar of sales.

Appendix

DOCUMENTS AND FORMS ARE INFORMATIONAL, NOT LEGAL ADVICE.

The forms and information available in this book are not intended as legal advice and should not be considered as such. They are provided for reference. The content and format of forms are not specifically determined by a statute or court rule and may require modification to suit specific facts of any different situation. The publication of these forms is in no way a representation that they are appropriate for use in a particular situation, or that they are adequate for use without modification and/or elaboration. In addition, the law may change at any time, making current forms outdated.

To ensure proper use of any of these forms or others you may need, consult a licensed attorney.

Checklist for Buyers (Short Form)

1. Call a buyer immediately.
2. Gently prequalify the buyer to determine which businesses are most suitable.
3. Send buyer to a lender or broker to obtain loan prequalification if necessary.
4. Send buyer to an immigration attorney to get prequalified for the E2 visa, if necessary.
5. Search for compatible businesses for the buyer.
6. Obtain signed NDAs from your buyer for each business of interested.
7. Send buyer an MLS business listing sheet for each business.
8. Call the listing agent and obtain further information including a memo and financials.
9. Send any memorandum or financial worksheets to buyer.
10. Send the signed NDA to the listing agent.
11. Call buyer back to discuss the information that you sent.
12. Get a business buyer's profile form prior to arranging meetings with sellers.
13. Try to get buyer to make an offer prior to a meeting with the seller.
14. Arrange a meeting between the buyer and seller.
15. If not done already, calculate a valuation for the business and try to get an offer.
16. Speak to the listing agent about the offer.
17. Submit an LOI or offer to purchase in writing.
18. Finalize negotiations and receive fully executed purchase agreement.
19. Arrange for an attorney to hold the escrow and handle the closing.
20. Assist your buyer with initiating and completing the due diligence process.
21. Obtain all necessary business licenses and permits.
22. Assist buyer with new credit accounts or transferring accounts from seller to buyer.
23. Arrange for an assignment of lease or a new lease.
24. Arrange for a final inventory prior to the closing.
25. After closing the seller has to train the buyer, they have to transfer the merchant account and POS system software, and account receivables/payables are adjusted in accordance with the closing agreement. Most of the time the sellers and buyers can handle these items on their own. Not always.

Business Buyer's Profile

Date: _____   Home Tel: _____

Name: _____   Office Tel: _____

Company: _____   Cell Phone: _____

Address: _____   Email: _____

City: _____

State: _____ Zip: _____

Background

Business Experience/Occupation: _____

Industries or Business Types Preferred: _____

Locations Preferred: _____

What technical or business skills do you possess? _____

Timing of Purchase: ☐ 1-6 months   ☐ 6-12 months   ☐ Just Looking

Do you want a franchise: ☐ Yes   ☐ No

Are you presently located in Florida or available to visit Florida with 14 days' notice?
☐ Yes   ☐ No

Price range of the business: _____ Minimum yearly salary required: _____

How will you finance your total investment? Cash: ____ Bank Loan: ____ Private Investor: ____

Financials

Cash Available: _____   Stocks or Other Liquid Derivatives:

Real Estate Equity: _____   _____

Company: _____   Other Investments: _____

                                   Other Income: _____

Would you like assistance with prequalifying for an SBA loan?:
☐ Yes   ☐ No

The information provided here will be kept in confidence by the brokerage and its agents. The information may be disclosed to sellers, sellers' agents, and other parties involved in a business purchase or negotiation.

Remember, your financial information makes sellers feel a lot more comfortable when opening their confidential financial records to you. Sellers may deal with as many as 30 different buyers (or choose not to) during a listing period, therefore, this information makes them more likely to deal with you.

The undersigned certifies that the information contained herein is true and correct.

Signature: _____   Date: _____

Buyer Broker Agreement

This Agreement made on the ____ day of ____, _____ is by and between: _____ (Buyer) and: _____ (Broker) and grants Broker the exclusive right to work with Buyer to locate and negotiate a purchase of a suitable business and/or real property. This Agreement ends on _____ , _____ . If Buyer enters into an Agreement to acquire a business or real property that is pending as of the date of termination, this agreement will continue until such transaction has closed or is otherwise terminated.

Property Description: Buyer is interested in a business and/or real property as follows:

Type of Business or Property: _____ Price Range: $ _____

Broker's Obligations: Broker will use its knowledge and skills:

1. Assist Buyer to purchase and financing the business or real property.

2. Discuss Buyer's investment needs and assist to locating suitable offerings from all sources.

3. Assist Buyer with Offers and contracts, monitor deadlines and Close resulting transactions.

4. Suggest, recommend and/or arrange for professional assistance for legal, tax, environmental, technical or immigration matters, whichever the case may be, to protect Buyer's interests. Broker is not authorized to give legal, financial, environmental, or other technical advice. Further, Broker does not warrant or guarantee goods or services provided by any third party whom Broker, at Buyer's request, refers Buyer to.

Buyer's Obligations: Buyer will cooperate with Broker:

1. Supplying accurate personal and financial information as requested by Broker.

2. To only use Broker to locate and negotiate opportunities and refer to Broker all inquiries received directly from owners, agents and other sources, and advise these parties that you are represented exclusively by Broker.

3. Indemnify and hold Broker harmless from all losses, damages, costs and expenses of any kind, including attorney's fees, and from any liabilities Broker may incur while acting on Buyer's behalf.

Compensation: Broker's compensation is earned during the term, extension or renewal of this Agreement when Buyer, or persons acting for or on behalf of Buyer, contracts to purchase or otherwise establish an interest in a business or real property as specified above. Buyer will pay to Broker the amount specified below but will be credited by any amount which Broker receives from a seller or another broker working for a seller. $ _____ or ____ %, whichever is greater, of the total purchase price or other considerations needed to acquire the property, to be paid at Closing.

Buyer Default: Broker's compensation will be due immediately upon Buyer's default in any contract to acquire property.

Protection Period: For a period of ____ days after the termination of this Agreement, if Buyer contracts to acquire a business or property brought to Buyer's attention by Broker, the compensation as described above, is due and payable on demand.

Early Termination: Buyer may cancel this Agreement at any time by written notice to Broker. However, for a time period matching the termination date shown plus the protection period, if Buyer acquires a business or real property, or an interest is same matching the "Type of Business or Property" specified, Broker's compensation as described hereon is due and payable upon demand. Broker may terminate this Agreement by written notice and Buyer will be released from all obligations under this Agreement.

Dispute Resolution: Any unresolved disputes between the parties will first be Mediated. If a settlement is not reached in mediation, the matter will be submitted to binding arbitration per the rules of the American Arbitration Association or another mutually agreed to Arbitrator.

Brokerage Relationship(s): Buyer authorizes Broker to operate as Single Agent ____ or Transaction Broker ____ Single Agent.

Buyer: _____   Broker: _____

_____   _____
Signature   Signature

Cooperative Brokerage Agreement (Buyer)

Dated: _____

This Agreement is by and between: _____ (Broker 1) and: _____ (Broker 2) concerning only the buyer described below. For consideration as hereafter expressed, the parties agree as follows:

1. Broker 2 acknowledges that Broker 1 has a "buyer" for a business to be found.

    Name of Buyer Here: _____

2. Broker 2 acknowledges having received information about the potential buyer from Broker 1.

3. The parties agree that if Broker 2 receives a commission on a sale of a business by said buyer, Broker 1 shall be entitled to a commission, if, as, or when received by the other Broker in the amount of Twenty Percent (20%) of such amount received.

4. The duration of this Agreement shall be one year.

5. Unless authorized by Broker 1, all appointments for showings, gathering data and contacts with the buyer shall be handled through Broker 1.

6. Broker 1, its agents and affiliates will not disclose the identity, availability for sale or any other information about prospective businesses to any party, other than with buyer. Broker 2 will require buyer to execute a "Standard Confidentiality Agreement" or similar device with regard to each prospective business.

7. This Agreement shall be governed by the laws of the State of Florida.

8. Each party agrees to share, in the same proportion as the commission is to be shared, all legal and related expenses of collection of any commission due and payable by reason of the buyer described above. If either party declines to pay said proportionate share of legal or related expenses as and when due, such party shall be deemed to have assigned to the other party all rights, title and interest in and to any commission that may be ultimately secured regarding the buyer.

9. This Agreement is not assignable by Broker 2. All assignments or attempted assignments by Broker 2, shall be deemed null and void and of no force and effect. Further, Broker 2 will not solicit or accept the cooperation of any other broker or similar party without the knowledge and approval of Broker 1.

10. Should any provisions hereof be deemed illegal or unenforceable, the other provisions hereof shall be given full effect separately therefrom and shall not be affected thereby.

11. This Agreement constitutes the entire agreement between the parties regarding said Business and there are no other agreements or understandings relating to the subject matter hereof between the parties. This Agreement cannot be changed, modified or amended except in writing signed by the parties.

12. In the event any party hereto institutes legal proceedings to enforce any provision of this Agreement, the prevailing party in such proceedings shall be entitled to reasonable attorney's fees as determined by the Court, in addition to all allowable court costs and expenses.

13. Both parties to this Agreement consent to cooperate fully in the sale to the buyer regarding showings, information, advertising, etc. Each party gives its covenant of good faith and fair dealings with respect to this Agreement.

Date: _____   Date: _____

_____   _____
Broker 1 Signature   Broker 2 Signature

Non-Circumvention & Non-Disclosure Agreement

This Non-Circumvention & Non-Disclosure Agreement, by and between: _____ its subsidiaries, principals, officers and employees whose primary address is _____ (herein after: "BROKER") and _____ whose address is _____ and its subsidiaries to include all principals, officers and employees (herein after: "BUYER"), dated _____.

Whereas the purpose of this Agreement is that BUYER desires to obtain Confidential Information from BROKER in order to evaluate, purchase or participate in OPPORTUNITY of BROKER and BROKER desires to provide BUYER the information needed to determine their initial purchase and continued purchase(s) of BROKER's OPPORTUNITY in accordance with the Definitions and Terms herein and with acknowledgement by BUYER that BROKER currently has Proprietary Working Relationships with contractual obligations to include Confidentiality and Non-Circumvention Agreements of which BROKER is contractually obligated and required to maintain confidentiality with third parties and should BUYER not adhere to this Agreement the effects my result have a Material Effect on BROKER's existing Proprietary Working Relationships of which such remedies, losses and repercussions can be passed on in full to BUYER in conjunction to other Remedies as stated herein, and

The Definitions below are mutually agreed to be necessary and adopted for purposes of this Agreement, and are:

"OPPORTUNITY" as used herein is defined as the opportunity to purchase and repurchase the following: _____
(Business Listing Number and Type of Business)

"Confidential Information" which is also proprietary, as used herein is defined as any written, electronic or oral communication consisting of one or more of the following:

a.   Any and all information relating to Opportunity

b.   proprietary information relating to the various operations, properties, personnel, financial and other matters which are non-public, confidential or proprietary in nature.

c.   Any and all analysis, compilations, studies or other material(s) provided to BUYER by or though BROKER.

"Non-Confidential Information" as used herein is defined as any written, electronic or oral communication of consisting of one or more of the following:

a. That information that is in the public domain at the time said information is provided by BROKER to BUYER,

b. Information that becomes part of the public domain through no efforts of BUYER after such time as provided by BROKER to BUYER,

c. Information independently developed by third parties not related or associated with BUYER,

"Permissible Disclosure(s)" as used herein is defined as any written, electronic or oral communication of consisting of one or more of the following:

a. Confidential Information to include this Agreement that BUYER is compelled to provide by way of laws, regulations, rules, order or legal processes or proceedings,

b. Those whom BUYER engages in the capacity of legal counsel, bankers, accountants or examiners of whom must have a fiduciary relationship with BUYER and must be made aware of this Agreement,

c. Those who have executed and a NON-CIRCUMVENTION & NON-DISCLOSURE AGREEMENT and have established a privite relationship with BROKER,

The Terms herein are mutually agreed to be necessary and adopted for purposes of this Agreement, and are:

The parties acknowledge that the Confidential Information is the property of BROKER, and the disclosure of the Confidential Information to BUYER does not convey any right, title or license in the Confidential Information to BUYER. BUYER shall not appropriate the Confidential Information to BUYER'S own use or to the use of any third party and shall only use the Confidential Information for the exclusive benefit of BUYER except to the extent otherwise authorized in writing by BROKER.

In return for agreeing to keep the information confidential, the BUYER has the right to receive the information from BROKER. The BUYER agrees not use the information for any purpose other than that set forth in the agreement and that money damages would not be sufficient remedy for any breach of this Agreement, and the non-breaching party shall be entitled to enforce this Agreement by ex-parte injunctive relief and other available relief, including equitable relief and monetary damages without limitation specific performance of BUYER.

BUYER will provide best efforts to ensure that anyone to whom the information is disclosed under the terms of this Agreement further abides by obligations restricting use, restricting disclosure, and ensuring security as protective as stated in this Agreement and to inform BROKER of any and all violations or potential violations.

For any and all third parties of which confidential information related to BROKER will or possibly be shared by or through BUYER, BUYER will execute this or similar "NON-CIRCUMVENTION & NON-DISCLOSURE AGREEMENT" which has been pre-approved by BROKER prior to any and all disclosures and said document will be provided to BROKER. BUYER acknowledges that non-performance of this action is a violation of this is a material violation of this Agreement.

That It is further understood and agreed that no failure or delay by BROKER in exercising any right, power or privilege under this Agreement shall not operate as a waiver, nor shall any single or partial exercise preclude any other or further exercise or the exercise of any right, power or privilege under this Agreement.

For two years from the date of this Agreement, BUYER agrees not to deal directly or indirectly with the Sellers of the OPPORTUNITY listed above without the prior written consent of BROKER. If BUYER enters into a sale and/or purchase agreement, a management contract or other financial arrangement with a Seller of an opportunity, including a leasing of the business premises from the Seller or its Landlord is consummated, BUYER shall be liable for any and all damages BROKER may suffer, including but not limited to the Seller's commission payable on the sales price or minimum commission due under the Listing Agreement with Seller, whichever is greater and, any commission due on the lease agreement negotiated with the Landlord. BUYER agrees and does hereby appoint BROKER its attorney in fact to execute all documents necessary to place a lien on the business assets to collect its compensation.

The binding term of this Agreement will be the longer of either one year from the last date of the signature provided below or one year from the most recent delivery of good or services of the BROKER to BUYER.

Communication – Any and all communication via email will be acceptable for purposes of this Agreement except for notice of modification or termination of this Agreement to which third party documented notice of delivery must be obtained by the sending party. Verbal communication is not acceptable for adherence purposes of changing or modifying this Agreement. Verbal communication is encompassed as a method that may be utilized in unauthorized disclosure of Confidential Information as referred to herein and constitutes a violation of this Agreement.

Any and all information provided to BUYER is provided for informational purposes only. BROKER does not make any representations and/or warranties as to the accuracy of the information provided and that BUYER is to make his or her own independent evaluation of the opportunities described above. BUYER acknowledges that BROKER has advised BUYER to seek independent professional advice in the review and evaluation of the information provided and that BUYER should seek the advice of an attorney and/or certified public accountant.

In the event BUYER discloses the availability of said designated opportunities to a third party who purchases a business without BROKER assistance, then BUYER, in addition to the remedies specified herein, is also responsible for payment of BROKER'S compensation which would have been paid on the listed selling price or minimum compensation, whichever is greater.

This Agreement shall be governed by and construed and interpreted in accordance with the substantive laws and jurisdiction governed in and by the State of _____, United States of America. Any disputes arising out of this Agreement shall be venued in federal or state district court in the State of _____ and each party hereby consents to the jurisdiction of such court.

Whole Agreement - Whenever possible, each provision of this Agreement shall be interpreted in such manner as to be effective and valid under applicable law as stated herein, but if any provision hereof shall be prohibited by or invalid under applicable law, such provision shall be ineffective to the extent of such prohibition or invalidity, without invalidating the remainder of such provision or the remaining provisions of this Agreement. All obligations of the BUYER and rights of the BROKER expressed in this Agreement shall be in addition to, and not in limitation of, those provided by applicable law. This Agreement may be executed in any number of counterparts, each of which shall be an original, but all of which together shall constitute one instrument. Any headings and or paragraph headings are for reference purposes only. Agreement shall be binding upon the parties and their successors and assigns.

IN WITNESS WHEREOF, this agreement has been executed as of the date first set forth above.

THIS IS A SAMPLE AGREEMENT TO BE USED FOR EDUCATIONAL PURPOSES ONLY AND NOT AS AN NDA FOR A BUSINESS TRANSACTION.

Letter Of Intent

Dated: _____

Title and Name: _____

Address: _____

_____

Dear _____:

This term sheet sets forth general terms and conditions of a proposed transaction between _____ in an acquiring company to be formed, (collectively "Buyer") and _____ and any related companies and shareholders (collectively "Seller").

1. **Real and Effective Acquisition.** Buyer would acquire substantially all of the assets, tangible and intangible, owned by Seller that are used in, or necessary for the conduct of its business.

2. **Consideration.** The aggregate consideration for the assets and business to be purchased would be $ _____. Paid as follows: Down payment: _____, Bank Financing: _____, Seller Financing: _____

3. **Due Diligence Review.** Promptly following the execution of this letter of intent, Seller will allow Buyer to complete an examination of financial, accounting and business records to complete due diligence. The parties will cooperate to complete due diligence expeditiously.

4. **Definitive Purchase Agreement.** All of the terms and conditions of the proposed transaction would be stated in the Purchase Agreement, to be negotiated, agreed and executed by Buyer and Seller.

5. **Exclusivity.** Seller will not solicit other proposals from other buyers for a period of 10 days from the date of this letter.

6. **Expediency.** All parties would use all reasonable efforts to complete and sign the Purchase Agreement on or before _____ and to close the transaction as promptly as practicable thereafter.

7. **Broker's Fees.** All parties have represented to each other that no brokers or finders have been employed who would be entitled to a fee by reason of the transaction contemplated by this letter of intent.

8. Other Conditions. _____

_____

_____

_____

If the foregoing terms and conditions are acceptable to you, please so indicate by signing the enclosed copy of this letter and returning it to the attention of the undersigned.

Sincerely,	**Accepted and Agreed**
[Buyer]	[Seller]
By: _____	By: _____
Title: _____	Title: _____

Free Cash Flow ROE and ROI

Company: ABC Company

ROE is Return on Equity

ROI is Return on Investment

Based on Asking Price

Free Cash Flow	
Profit	124,550
Free Cash Flow	95,107
Max Loan on FCF	637,219
Prices	
Business Selling Price	260,000
Multiple Price / FCF	2.73
Building Selling Price	0
Rent	12,000
Multiple Price / Rent	0.00
Total Prices	260,000
Assets	
FFE	60,000
Building	0
Goodwill	200,000
Total Assets	260,000
Loans	
i	6%
n	10
LTV	85%
FFE	221,000
Building	0
Total Loans	221,000
Buyer	
Buyer's contribution	39,000
Buyer's contribution %	15%
Loans PMT Yearly	($29,442.64)
ROE on FCF, including all loan PMTs	244%
ROI on FCF	37%

FCF has been reduced by any loan payments indicated below

Buyer contributes $39,000 towards the purchase price to receive $95,107 each year in FCF.

Buyer is on the hook for $260,000 and will receive $95,107 each year in FCF.

Checklist for Sellers (Short Form)

1. Answer your phone or call sellers back immediately, it's your best chance to make contact.

2. Arrange to see the seller's business as soon as possible, it's your best chance to get in front of them to make presentations. Strike while the iron is hot, as the saying goes.

3. Ask the seller to have financial information available so you can evaluate if the business is worth your while. If the financials are not in order, you may not want the listing.

4. The first meeting is to see if you want the listing and educate sellers about the sales process.

5. Obtain a signed retainer agreement and then instruct the seller to gather all of the data necessary for the listing.

6. Create a valuation report and a comprehensive offering memorandum. This process can take some time with many calls and interviews with sellers.

7. Submit the business financials to a bank for SBA prequalification.

8. Arrange a meeting to review the valuation report, offering memorandum, and to discuss pricing and marketing.

9. Have the seller sign a marketing agreement.

10. Market the business by placing the listing in the local business MLS, on commercial business sales websites, and in newspapers or trade journals as necessary. You can also call or mail potential businesses to see if they are interested in buying the listing.

11. Update the listing monthly or as you receive new information and new financials.

12. Screen buyers to obtain the necessary pre-qualifications to purchase the business prior to arranging a meeting with your seller.

13. Conduct meetings efficiently. Don't waste time with buyers who are just looking.

14. Get all offers in writing.

15. Make counter-offers quickly so as not to lose buyers (buyer's remorse).

16. Upon obtaining a signed purchase agreement, arrange for an attorney or closing agent to hold the escrow money and handle the closing.

17. Make sure due diligence starts and finishes in accordance with the purchase agreement.

18. Assist buyers with applying for financing, any necessary licenses, the assignment of the lease, arrange an inventory accounting if necessary, and assist with the transfer of the merchant account if necessary.

19. After closing is completed, you can arrange for the seller and buyer to meet to work out a schedule for training.

Required Information

Information Needed for Valuation

- Tax returns (3-5 yrs) with associated P&L statements
- Monthly P&L since last Tax Return
- List of Furniture, Fixtures, & Equipment (note age and est. of fair market value)
- Estimated values of inventory at cost and at fair market value
- Estimated value and list of other assets (i.e. Autos, tools, patents)
- Completed Seller Information Worksheet or I can interview you

Other Information

Financial

- Breakdown of sales by month (3 yrs)
- Breakdown of annual sales for top 10 customers (3 yrs)
- Copy of franchise agreement (if any)
- Details of corporate contracts (if any)

Product/Margins

- Segmentation of yearly gross sales by products and service (3 yrs)
- List your profit margins by segmentation of products and service

Assets

- List of all assets and estimated market values
- Copy of vehicle registrations — note mileage and condition

Liabilities

- Schedule of accounts payable
- Description of all notes, mortgages, equipment leases, and other liabilities

Staff (This information can be listed in the Seller Information Worksheet)

- List of employees by name, tenure, function, wage/salary, # hrs. worked
- List of owners by name, job title, function, hours worked, and salary
- Description of employee benefits
- Description of owner's benefits and amounts (IRA, Insurance, auto, phone, etc.)

Premises

- Copy of premise lease and addenda (extensions)
- Copy of Business Tax Receipt (occupancy license)
- If real estate is owned- copy of plot plan, survey, and recent tax bill

Insurance

- Copy of declaration page of all business policies

Industry Information

- Copy of any necessary licenses and permits for the business and operators
- Copy of Company promotional material
- Pictures of work area or any pertinent part of business or assets

Engagement Letter - No Retainer Fee

Dated: _____

Dear Seller:

In Consideration of Florida Business Brokers (Business Advisor), providing Financial Advisory, Marketing, Brokerage and other Advisory Services to Client located at Client Address (Seller) relating to the sale of Client (Company), Client Address.

The Seller and Business Advisor contract as follows:

1. APPOINTMENT: The Seller hereby employs and appoints Business Advisor as the SOLE AND EXCLUSIVE AGENT with SOLE AND EXCLUSIVE RIGHT TO SELL Company, including all furniture, equipment, fixtures, inventory, goodwill, debt or liability assumption, trademarks and trade names, commencing with your acceptance of this Agreement, which will continue for a period of twelve (12) months from the date marketing efforts begin as authorized by Seller.

2. ACCEPTANCE: Business Advisor hereby accepts employment and promises to use its best efforts in Business Advisor's ordinary course of business to offer for sale and to procure a ready, willing and able purchaser for the Company described above. Seller hereby authorizes Business Advisor to present any and all offers Business Advisor may receive. Business Advisor, it's agents, or any escrow agent he designates are authorized to accept deposits and issue receipts for deposits on all offers.

3. THE ASSIGNMENT: Business Advisor agrees to provide the following services to Seller in two phases as described below.

Phase 1 as authorized by executing this agreement:

a. Profile Company's past and present operating performance and obtain an understanding of future operating prospects.

b. Analyze Company's past and present financial statements and prepare projections as may be required to predict future results.

c. Develop, within fourteen (14) days after receipt of all required information from Seller, a Business Marketing Evaluation with Buyer Identification report including compilations, recasting, ratio analysis, industry comparison (when applicable) and analysis of all financial and operating information for review and approval of Seller prior to commencing marketing efforts.

Phase 2 as authorized by executing the Addendum, "Authorization to Commence Marketing Efforts".

d. Once Seller has agreed on proposed price and terms by separate Addendum, identify appropriate prospective purchasers qualified to acquire Company and prepare materials as may be appropriate to be used in presenting the Company to prospective purchasers.

e. Negotiate the terms and conditions of a merger or sale on terms and conditions acceptable to Seller.

f. Provide continuing advisory services to Seller, its accounting firm and legal advisors as may be required to consummate the merger or sale of the Company.

4. HOLD HARMLESS: The Seller understands and hereby acknowledges that all facts, figures and other information and all additional supporting documentation pertaining to the Business, have been provided to Business Advisor by Seller, and that Business Advisor will rely upon Seller's representations of such facts, figures, suitability of equipment and other information when describing and promoting the Business to potential purchasers, without making an investigation into the accuracy and completeness of such representations by Seller. Therefore, Seller hereby represents and warrants that all such facts, figures, suitability of equipment and other information provided are true and complete in all material respects and warrants that all such facts, figures, suitability of equipment and other information provided are true and complete in all material respects and contain no material omissions. Seller hereby agrees to indemnify and hold harmless Business Advisor against any and all claims, demands, causes for all action, losses, damages, cost and expenses, including reasonable attorney's fees and fees on appeals arising out of a breach of this warranty, and further agrees that Palm Beach County is proper venue for any such action or suit in connection with any misrepresentations or omissions made by or on behalf of Seller relative to the Business.

5. COMPENSATION: Seller agrees to pay Business Advisor, as consideration for Business Advisor's services:

a. Seller agrees to pay a Transaction Fee to Business Advisor by certified check or attorney escrow check at the closing according to the following "Modern Lehman" formula: 10% of the first $1 million, plus

    • 9% of the second $1 million, plus

    • 8% of the third $1 million, plus

    • 7% of the fourth $1 million, plus

- 6% of the fifth $1 million, plus
- 5% of the sixth $1 million, plus
- 4% of the seventh $1 million, plus
- 3% of everything above $8 million.

6. THE TRANSACTION FEE is fully earned by Business Advisor if: a) the Transaction as proposed in the Addendum Authorization to Commence Marketing Efforts or on any other terms acceptable to the Seller (whether it is a lease, sale, trade, transfer, or other disposition of Company, Company shares, or Company assets) is consummated during the term of this Agreement (including any extensions), or b) within eighteen months thereafter with a purchaser with whom Business Advisor and/or the Seller has had discussions relating to the Transaction during the term of this Agreement, or c) once marketing efforts have been authorized by the Seller, it decides not to sell the Company or the Seller or its owners take some action which would prevent Business Advisor from selling the Company or consummating the Transaction.

7. The Seller authorizes and agrees that Broker, in its sole discretion, may co-broke with other brokers or may refuse to do so. The Seller authorizes Broker to cooperate with any other brokers regardless of their Agency Status. In doing so Broker, at its sole discretion, may share all or any portion of the total commission with such other brokers.

8. The Seller authorizes Broker and any other broker with whom Broker is co-operating, to disclose Seller's reasons for the sale of the Business to any Buyer or Prospect.

9. DEFINITIONS: Total Consideration, for purposes of this Agreement, shall be defined as, but not limited to, any cash; securities; credit arrangements or any other property controlled by the Company or Seller, its shareholders or officers; assumption of Company or Seller liabilities; assets; promissory notes; face value of obligations arising from employment agreements, covenants not to compete, equipment lease contracts; and any other like arrangements intended to convey value in connection with the Transaction.

10. ADVERTISING: The Seller agrees that upon consummation of the Transaction contemplated herein Business Advisor, may at its expense, advertise its role in effecting the transaction.

11. This Agreement contains the entire understanding between the parties. Any change or modification must be in writing and signed by the parties.

12. This Agreement shall be governed by the laws of the state of Florida. If any dispute arises out of this Agreement, the breach or the interpretation thereof, the parties may seek a resolution by sharing the cost of non-binding mediation, per the "Florida Mediation Act Chapter 44." If, however, a resolution by binding arbitration, in accordance with the rules of the American Arbitration Association, or by litigation is unavoidable, the Arbitrator/Court is instructed to award the expenses of the arbitration/trial, including reasonable attorney's fees and costs to the prevailing party. A judgment and awards shall be entered by a court of competent jurisdiction. The parties further agree that jurisdiction and venue for any conflict and the entry of judgments shall be in Palm Beach County, Florida.

I have read and understood, and hereby agree to the above terms and provisions of the Agreement and the Addendum hereto, and hereby acknowledge receipt of a copy of this Agreement and Addendum. Also, I represent and warrant that the undersigned constitute all of the owners/partners/shareholders of the Seller listed herein and hereby personally guarantee performance of this Agreement.

Sincerely yours,

Florida Business Brokers

_____   Dated: _____
William Thomas, President

Confirmed and Accepted

Client

_____   Dated: _____
Seller, President

Authorization to Commence Marketing

By this addendum, Florida Business Brokers is authorized to commence efforts to sell that business known as: Client (Company) located client Address

Proposed Terms of Sale:

Down Payment $ _____   Balance by Note $ _____

Assumable Debt $ _____   Total Purchase Price $ _____

Other $ _____

Seller will carry balance at $ _____ per month including ____% interest on unpaid balance, secured by assets being sold and personal guarantee of buyer.

Inventory:

Approximate Inventory at time of sale, valued at cost, to be included in Total Purchase Price:

$ _____ (The Down Payment or Notes to Seller will be adjusted by any variance.)

Not Included in Sale: _____

Training:

Owner(s) agree to train a buyer for ____ days at no cost and thereafter for ____ days at a cost of $ ____.

Covenants:

Owner(s) agree not to compete with purchaser in a similar business for ____ months within a ____ mile radius of the company location. Owner agrees to train purchaser for a period of ____ days as part of the purchase price.

Lease:

Owner warrants the transferability of the existing lease or a new lease at $ ____ per month for ____ remaining months and ____ renewal option(s) of ____ years.

This Addendum is part of that Marketing Agreement dated _____

Seller: _____ Date: _____

Open Listing Agreement

Name of Brokerage: _____

Address: _____

In consideration of the services of (Name of brokerage) hereinafter referred to as the Broker, for a period of 180 days from the date hereon, I hereby grant the Broker the right to show my/our business known as: _____
with an Address of: _____
and offer it "For Sale" at the following asking PRICE: $ _____ and
TERMS: _____

_____

I/We agree to pay the Broker a commission of Ten percent (10%) of the final selling price, with a minimum commission of _____ Dollars ($ _____), should they sell my/our business, or cause a transaction to be done, within 180 days of the date of this Agreement at the PRICE and TERMS shown above, or any other PRICE and/or TERMS acceptable to me/us.

Should the Owner(s) sell to a Buyer not registered hereon, no commission is due the Broker. Broker shall obtain a signed non-disclosure agreement for each Buyer the Broker shows the business. A signed non-disclosure agreement shall attest that the Buyer is a registered buyer in accordance with the registration provision herein.

SIGNED and AGREED to on _____.

Broker is represented by: _____

Name: _____

Owner: _____

Name: _____

Cooperative Brokerage Agreement

Dated: _____

This Agreement is by and between: _____ (Broker 1)
and: _____ (Broker 2) concerning only the business
described below. For consideration as hereafter expressed, the parties agree as
follows:

1. Broker 2 acknowledges that Broker 1 has a "potential listing" on the business
   or property now described (the Business) Description Here:

   _____

   Broker 2 acknowledges having received information about the Business from
   Broker 1.

2. The parties agree that if Broker 2 receives a commission on the sale of the
   Business, the Broker 1 shall be entitled to a commission, if, as, or when received
   by Broker 2 in the amount of Fifty Percent (20%) of such amount received.

3. The duration of this Agreement shall coincide with the term of a listing agreement regarding the Business.

4. Unless authorized by Broker 1, all appointments for showing the Business,
   gathering data and contacts with the principals of the Business or their agents,
   employees, suppliers, creditors, etc., shall be handled through Broker 1.

5. Broker 2, its agents and affiliates will not disclose the identity, availability
   for sale or any other information about the Business to any party, other than
   those qualified prospective buyers procured by Broker 2. Broker 2 will require any prospective purchaser to execute a "Confidentiality Agreement" or
   similar device provided by or acceptable to Broker 1 and will supply Broker
   1 with such executed copy and with a copy of a signed personal or corporate
   financial statement. Broker 1 reserves the right of final approval with respect
   to any prospective buyer, which approval shall not be unreasonably withheld.

6. This Agreement shall be governed by the laws of the State of _____.

7. Each party agrees to share, in the same proportion as the commission is to
   be shared, all legal and related expenses of collection of any commission due
   and payable by reason of the listing agreement described above. If either
   party declines to pay said proportionate share of legal or related expenses as
   and when due, such party shall be deemed to have assigned to the other party

all rights, title and interest in and to any commission that may be ultimately secured regarding the listing.

8. This Agreement is not assignable by Broker 2. All assignments or attempted assignments by Broker 2, shall be deemed null and void and of no force and effect. Further, Broker 2 will not solicit or accept the cooperation of any other broker or similar party without the knowledge and approval of Broker 1.

9. Should any provisions hereof be deemed illegal or unenforceable, the other provisions hereof shall be given full effect separately therefrom and shall not be affected thereby.

10. This Agreement constitutes the entire agreement between the parties regarding said Business and there are no other agreements or understandings relating to the subject matter hereof between the parties. This Agreement cannot be changed, modified or amended except in writing signed by the parties.

11. In the event any party hereto institutes legal proceedings to enforce any provision of this Agreement, the prevailing party in such proceedings shall be entitled to reasonable attorney's fees as determined by the Court, in addition to all allowable court costs and expenses.

12. Both parties to this Agreement consent to cooperate fully in the sale of the Business regarding showings, information, advertising, etc. Each party gives its covenant of good faith and fair dealings with respect to this Agreement.

Date: _____   Date: _____

_____   _____
Broker 1 Signature   Broker 2 Signature

Confidential Seller Registration Form

Dated: _____

Background

Name of Company _____

Address _____

_____

Telephone _____ Fax _____

E Mail Address _____ Web Address _____

Name and Home Address of All Shareholders and Percentage of Ownership

_____

_____

_____

_____

Cell Phone and E-Mail address of Principal Shareholder _____

_____

Corporation Status   S Corp ____   C Corp ____   Other ____

Accountants _____ Telephone _____

Memo:

_____

_____

_____

_____

1. Brief History of Company, including;

A. Date and State of Incorporation: _____

B. States Qualified to do Business: _____

C. Licenses or necessary qualifications: _____

_____

_____

D. General Description of Company Services & Products and evolution thereof:

_____

_____

_____

E. When was company started or what year acquired by present owner? _____

F. How many years has this business been at this location? _____

2. Litigation

_____

_____

_____

_____

3. EPA Issues
(Status of Phase I, Superfund, in ground oil tanks, violations)

_____

_____

_____

_____

4. OSHA Violations

_____

_____

_____

_____

5. What would an absentee owner have to pay a manager annually, including all benefits and bonuses, to run this business profitably?

_____

6. What is the current market value of owned equipment and fixtures?

_____

Do not exceed original cost when adding salvage value.

7. What is the current market value of your leasehold improvements?

_____

Buyers will not pay for used leasehold improvements if they can get a new "build out" for free in a similar space.

8. What is the market value of included vehicles?

_____

List all vehicles separately.

9. What is the average daily value of stocks, supplies or merchandise for consumption or resale?

_____

Use monthly value if that is easier.

10. What will be the cost per square foot per month including all related fees on the average during the next three (3) years?

_____

11. Give the current lease rate per square foot per month for a similar space on this side of the street. _____

12. If any leased/purchase equipment value can be transferred, what is the difference between market value and current payoff? _____

13. What is the current market value of any transferable licenses, right or patents that will be sold with this business?

_____

If the right cannot be transferred legally, there is no asset value.

Use the following criteria to determine license or permit worth:

- Similar permits are currently available, and these permits have no expiration date: use the current replacement cost and add acquisition costs.

- Similar permits are currently available, and these permits have a definite expiration date:
    - Enter the fee to obtain this legal right
    - Divide cost by months permitted for use
    - Equals value per month
    - Time months held since issuance
    - Equals consumed value
    - Enter the fee to obtain this legal right
    - Deduct consumed value
    - Equals current residual value

- Information or data bases are generally valued by:
    - What was the original cost to create it?
    - What would it cost to replace today?
    - Where else is this data available at what cost?
    - What percent of revenue uses this data directly?
    - What percent of data is annually obsolete?
- Licenses, patents, unique permits, dealerships, copyrights, and similar legal rights are valued by security and income generation. Price can be determined by the following method:
- Research the local market for recently sold permits or right and uses of the trend of prices.

Critical Success Factors

1. What factors are critical to your success and drive growth?
(i.e. proprietary products, management, customer service, price etc.)

_____

_____

_____

_____

2. How would you grow the business?

_____

_____

_____

_____

Products And Services

1. As you review the past 12 months, what percent of total revenues came is as green cash? Do not count anything but pure cash.

_____

2. What percentage of supplies or inventory for resale would be considered by an expert as dead or obsolete?

_____

"Dead Stock" can be defined as:

- Broken lots of goods in a retail store
- Disorganized storage of materials
- Obsolete parts or merchandise
- Normal bad stock levels will range from 5% in a very well-run organization to as much as 40% in a poorly managed shop.

3. Product and Service Line — Leading services or products in order of importance indicating % of contribution to profits. Indicate any brand names or special relationships with vendors.

_____
_____
_____
_____

4. Warranty costs yearly and policy

_____
_____

Marketing And Sales

1. Nature of Customers

_____
_____

2. Number of active customers

_____
_____

3. List of leading customers, showing the percentage amount of sales to each

_____
_____
_____
_____

4. Sales Personnel—How many in house sales persons and method of compensation?

_____
_____

5. What areas do you market?

_____

_____

Competition

1. Who are the primary competitors?

_____

_____

2. How does your company stand in comparison to competitors?
(size, quality, loyalty, years in business, etc.)

_____

_____

3. How secure are revenues?

_____

_____

- This question is directed at the cost of collections and the residual value of goods or services if repossessed.

- Trade Accounts: These are accounts receivable customers that purchase or receive good or services from a company and use or distribute the product in such a way that repossession is virtually impossible.

- Trade Accounts with easy repossession: These accounts are similar to the first category, but your product or service can be repossessed easily.

- Lien able trade accounts, charge cards or checks: Accounts receivable in this category are backed by lien or attachment laws that assist in collections. In some states a lien can be filed against the title or deed to property thereby requiring payment at the time of sale of the property. Checks and charge cards do not insure collection; therefore, a loss of some level is generally incurred.

- Trade accounts with bank collateral value: If this company trades with extremely stable or reliable customer (ATT, IBM, EXXON, etc.) collection is generally assured and such receivable can be collateralized instead of factored.

- Cash and cash only!

4. How many direct competitors are in this company's trade area?

_____

_____

Industry Trend

1. What is your liability exposure level?

_____

_____

- There is nothing mechanical, sharp or heavy in the work place.
- This work requires some light lifting, most sharp objects are protected or manually operated and there are no hazardous products.
- Some safety training and good common sense is required to prevent injuries.
- Minor injuries are almost daily with major injuries periodically.
- Safety in this work place requires formal training and fatalities or long-term health problems occur in this industry.

2. If you use the last three years as a trend, how have gross revenues been trending?

_____

_____

- Severe drop
- Mild recession decline
- Essentially flat
- Slight but definite growth after discounting inflation
- Growth beyond local or national inflation rates

3. This company gets most of its new business by what means?

_____

_____

4. How has this company's liability insurance rates gone?

_____

5. Give the trend of the market for this product?

_____

_____

Answers should represent activity over the past three (3) years and in this company's trading area.

    1.   Severe decline, many failures.

    2.   O.K.

    3.   This business is HOT.

6. How long has this industry or product been widely known?

_____

_____

7. Given this type of business, how would you rate this location for doing this type of business?

_____

_____

8. What is the local labor market like for this business?

_____

_____

9. What is the strength of Unions in this area and industry?

_____

_____

Facilities

1. For each facility—

A. Square footage: _____

B. Terms of leases: _____

C. Renewal provisions: _____

D. Features—door height, loading docks, etc: _____

E. Rent with escalations and expense pass thru's: _____

F. Parking: _____

H. If owned, is it included in sale or available for sale: _____

Manufacturing

1. Raw materials

_____
_____

2. Manufacturing process

_____
_____
_____
_____

3. Justification of inventory level maintained

_____
_____
_____
_____

4. At what capacity is plant operating?

_____
_____

5. Days and hours of operations

_____
_____

Equipment

1. List primary equipment and estimated value.

_____
_____

2. Given the current state of leasehold improvements and equipment, what percent will need to be replaced each year to maintain a good image and run efficiently?

- Divide the estimated value of assets by the total estimated annual costs.

- Divide the maintenance expenses by the book value of all assets.

Employees

1. Number of employees by function or department - include salary range or labor rate.

---

2. Benefit plans for employees (401K, medical benefits, pensions etc.).

Management And Ownership

1. For all management personnel, please list: name, position, time w/ company, age, compensation including bonus, and prior experience, if significant.

---

2. How many family members, relatives and/or partners, including the owner, are actively working in this business?

_____

_____

3. How important is the owner to the revenue of this business?

_____

_____

- The owner is the business
- The owner controls all activities
- The owner makes all major decisions
- The owner shows up periodically
- Nobody is sure who the owner is

4. Given an individual with reasonable skills and little direct knowledge of this business, how long would it take to functionally learn this business?

_____

_____

"Functionally means the ability to maintain the current level of activity with modest growth and handling all routine problems.

5. What amount of training is required to understand and perform most phases of this company's operations?

_____

_____

1. Days
2. Weeks
3. Months or technical training required
4. Years or college curriculum required
5. College equivalent and national certification

6. How much owner training time would-be given to a buyer at no charge?

_____

_____

Shareholder/Owner Signature: _____

Seller's Discretionary Earnings Worksheet

Company: ABC Company   **Period Covered:**

	Tax Returns or P&L	(Adjustment Amount)	Reason for Adjustment	Adjusted Amount
Sales				
Gross Sales	1,500,000	200,000	Sales from unrelated business	1,300,000
Cost of Goods Sold	589,000			589,000
Gross Profit	911,000			711,000
			Adjusted Gross Profit	711,000

	Tax Returns or P&L	(Adjustment Amount)	Reason for Adjustment	Adjusted Amount
Expenses				
Accounting	1,200			1,200
Advertising	3,000			3,000
Amortization	0			0
Auto Expenses	15,000	3,850	Owner's personal auto lease	11,150
Bad Debt	0			0
Bank Charges	150			150
Commissions	0			0
Contract Labor	76,000			76,000
Depreciation	6,520	6,520	EBITDA is removed for SDE calc.	0
Donations	0			0
Dues-Subscriptions	325			325
Employee Benefits	0			0
Freight	0			0
Insurance - Business	2,500			2,500
Insurance - Auto	6,500	1,250	Owner's personal auto	5,250
Insurance - Health	50,000	10,000		40,000
Interest	6,300		EBITDA is removed for SDE calc.	6,300
Janitorial	600			600
Legal	1,500			1,500
Licenses	369			369
Maintenance	2,100			2,100
Office Supplies	9,400			9,400

	Tax Returns or P&L	(Adjustment Amount)	Reason for Adjustment	Adjusted Amount
Owner's Salary	100,000	100,000	Owner's benefit	0
Postage	3,500			3,500
Rent Equipment	6,789			6,789
Rent Facility	32,500			32,500
Repairs	1,500			1,500
Salaries	89,650			89,650
Supplies	1,000			1,000
Tax	0			0
Tax - Payroll	9,600			9,600
Telephone	5,000			5,000
Travel & Entertainment	9,600	9,600	Owner's family cruise	0
Utilities	9,850			9,850
Miscellaneous	500			500
			Total Adjusted Expenses	319,733

Adjusted Gross Profit	711,000
(minus) Total Adjusted Expenses	319,733
SDE - Seller's Discretionary Earnings	391,267

Multi-Year Comparison of SDE (Seller's Discretionary Earnings)

Company: ABC Company   **How many months of YTD?: 10**

	2017 YTD as of 10/30/2017	2017 Proforma	2016	2015	2014
Gross Sales					
Design	44,515	53,418	33,939	29,042	28,565
Freight	205,115	246,138	133,619	117,240	77,901
Install	124,706	149,647	174,377	264,817	58,911
Product	857,226	1,028,671	1,258,369	1,252,970	595,825
Refund/Discount	(16,031)	(19,237)	(51,661)	(80,368)	(21,388)
	1,215,531	**1,458,637** 100%	**1,548,643** 100%	**1,583,701** 100%	**739,814** 100%
COGS Subs	135,456	162,547	160,738	248,388	66,672
COGS Brokers	61,250	73,500	45,921	43,896	17,421
COGS Freight	8,425	10,110	61,943	36,869	25,801
COGS Purchases	489,500	587,400	709,942	620,746	279,161
COGS Other	6,706	8,047	5,111	3,140	8,091
Total COGS	**701,337**	**841,604** 58%	**983,655** 64%	**953,039** 60%	**397,146** 54%
Gross Profit	**514,194**	**617,033** 42%	**564,988** 36%	**630,662** 40%	**342,668** 46%

	2017 YTD as of 10/30/2017	2017 Proforma	2016	2015	2014
Expenses					
Accounting	0	0	0	0	5,851
Advertising	32,478	38,974	36,258	15,617	18,897
Amortization	0	0	0	0	0
Auto Expenses	11,458	13,750	16,025	11,470	11,259
Bad Debt	0	0	0	0	0
Bank Charges	0	0	0	0	0
Commissions	12,048	14,458	40,972	0	2,780
Contract Labor	44,321	53,185	8,533	30,697	0
Computer/Web	91	109	2,904	389	260
Discounts	0	0	0	0	0
Dues-Subscriptions	4,589	5,507	4,666	1,930	5,438
Employee Benefits	1,168	1,402	1,214	0	0
Equipment Rent	0	0	992	0	0
Gifts	3,215	3,858	2,520	10,452	1,540
Insurance - Business	2,576	3,091	3,110	2,597	2,196

	2017 YTD as of 10/30/2017	2017 Proforma	2016	2015	2014
Insurance - Auto	4,487	5,384	5,005	3,194	2,832
Insurance - Health	0	0	0	0	2,471
Interest	0	0	0	0	0
Janitorial	0	0	0	0	0
Legal	0	0	3,025	34,387	8,942
Licenses	304	365	15,597	18,566	5,915
Merchant Services	3,226	3,871	7,034	5,615	4,363
Office Expenses	10,579	12,695	10,028	2,435	6,458
Office Supplies	2,378	2,854	4,658	4,855	0
Postage	305	366	8,111	3,655	1,107
Printing	1,734	2,081	2,489	874	0
Rent Facility	58,815	70,578	74,792	39,751	52,633
Repairs	3,242	3,890	6,409	2,168	5,156
Salaries	84,569	101,483	78,733	99,414	56,398
Security	0	0	0	0	0
Tax	0	0	0	0	925
Tax - Payroll	14,164	16,997	3,219	3,605	0
Telephone	0	0	10,349	11,765	11,357
Meals & Entertainment	2,522	3,026	4,098	1,596	1,586
Travel	45,991	55,189	18,499	29,877	4,838
Utilities	9,564	11,477	2,481	992	1,987
Miscellaneous	3,856	4,627	360	1,822	1,484
	357,680	429,216	372,081	337,723	216,673
Adjusted Gross Profit		617,033 / 42%	564,988 / 36%	630,662 / 40%	342,668 / 46%
Total Adjusted Expenses		429,216 / 29%	372,081 / 24%	337,723 / 21%	216,673 / 29%
Total Owner's Profit		187,817 / 13%	192,907 / 12%	292,939 / 18%	125,995 / 17%

Add Backs Removed From Above					
Owner's Salary	63,696	76,435	135,456	200,000	55,000
Interest	8,268	9,922	8,502	10,643	17,127
Depreciation	0	0	15,574	0	1,165
Amortization	0	0	0	0	0
Owner's Pension	0	0	0	0	6,500
Personal Insurance	4,148	4,978	1,904	0	3,335
Commission Owner	6,000	7,200	0	0	0

Business Asset Purchase Agreement

Dated: _____

THIS AGREEMENT is made and entered into by:

      A. SELLER's Name, Address and Telephone No.: ("SELLER"); and

      B. BUYER's Name, Address and Telephone No.: ("BUYER").

SELLER agrees to sell to BUYER, and BUYER agrees it will purchase from SELL-
ER all of SELLER's assets and properties pertaining to the business known as
_____, located at _____. The assets
to be conveyed to BUYER by SELLER at the closing include all inventory, customer records, materials, supplies, equipment, machinery, leasehold improvements,
furniture, furnishings, fixtures, transferable licenses, business name, telephone
numbers, leasehold interest, goodwill, and other assets and intangibles used in
the business. This sale does not include the SELLER'S, accounts receivable, cash
on hand and _____.

PURCHASE PRICE

$ _____The Purchase Price.

PAYMENT OF PURCHASE PRICE

$ _____ Earnest Money Deposit paid by BUYER and being held by
_____.

$_____ Other Money Deposit paid on _____ and being held
by _____.

$ _____ **TOTAL DOWN PAYMENT**

$ _____ Bank Financing in such amount to payable DOLLARS
($_____) per month at an interest rate of percent (___%) per annum.

$_____Promissory Note to SELLER, bearing interest at _____ percent
(___%) per annum, amortized in equal installments of principal and interest
of DOLLARS ($_____) over (___) months. Payable to SELLER and
deliverable at closing.

$ _____ Cashier's Check or wire transfer payable to Closing Agent at or before closing.

$ _____ **TOTAL PURCHASE PRICE.**

ACCEPTANCE OF OFFER AND COUNTEROFFER

BUYER's offer shall remain open for SELLER's written acceptance on or before: _____ o'clock _____ M on _____ _____, _____ SELLER shall accept this offer by executing this Agreement and deliver to Broker. If SELLER fails to accept BUYERs Offer, at BUYER's option, the earnest money deposit shall be returned to BUYER and this offer withdrawn. Unless otherwise stated, the time for acceptance of any counteroffer shall be _____ (___) business days excluding any holidays.

CLOSING DATE

The undersigned hereby agree to execute any and all documents necessary to close this transaction. The Closing Date for this sale shall be on or about _____
_____, _____.

LIABILITIES

BUYER shall assume: _____
_____
_____

THIRD PARTY FINANCING

This Agreement is contingent upon third party financing; therefore: BUYER shall make written application to lender within _____ (___) days of the Effective Date of this Agreement. BUYER shall have _____ (___) days from the Effective Date of this Agreement to receive a written loan commitment on terms acceptable to BUYER and to BUYER's sole discretion. BUYER shall provide written notification to SELLER of BUYER's intent to close this transaction if lender's terms are acceptable to BUYER. BUYER may cancel this Agreement by written notice to SELLER and Broker within the loan commitment period; failure of BUYER to so notice the SELLER and Broker shall constitute BUYER's absolute waiver of this provision. BUYER's cancellation of this Agreement for the failure of a loan commitment shall cause this Agreement to be a nullity in all respects and particulars and vest the Escrow Agent with the authority to immediately refund any and all deposits held for this Agreement.

WARRANTIES AND REPRESENTATIONS OF SELLER

SELLER warrants and represents that at the closing, all sales taxes, interest and penalties which may be owing to the _____ Department of Revenue will have been paid and satisfied in full. Following the closing, SELLER agrees to indemnify the BUYER and hold the BUYER harmless from any and all sales taxes, interest and penalties that may be asserted against the BUYER as a result of the activities of SELLER prior to the closing.

SELLER also represents to BUYER that:
- SELLER is the owner of and has good and marketable title to all of the assets, free and clear of any liens, encumbrances or claims whatsoever, except as set forth in Section 6 above with respect to the existing obligations (if any) to be assumed by BUYER.
- SELLER possesses all licenses necessary to operate the business being transferred to BUYER.
- There are no judgments, liens, actions or proceedings pending or threatened by or against SELLER.
- The business of SELLER will be conducted up to the date of closing in accordance with all laws, rules and regulations, and SELLER will operate and maintain the business in regular course and not violate the terms of any Agreements with third parties.

MANAGEMENT ASSISTANCE

SELLER agrees to provide assistance to BUYER to transfer management and operation of the business during normal business hours at the location of the business for a period of _____ (___) days following the closing, all without additional consideration payable by BUYER to SELLER.

COVENANT NOT TO COMPETE

SELLER, including all officers, directors and shareholders of SELLER if SELLER is a corporation, will not directly or indirectly engage in or become interested in a similar business or any business or activity incidental to the business being purchased or become the agent or employee of any competitor of BUYER, or in any other way compete with BUYER, other than employment of the SELLER by the BUYER at the Business, within an area encompassing a radius of _____ (___)miles from the location of the Business for a period of _____ (___) years from the Closing Date. SELLER acknowledges that any remedy at law for breach of this covenant would be inadequate and that BUYER will be entitled to injunctive relief to enforce this Section, in addition to any other legal remedies available to BUYER for such breach of this Section. SELLER acknowledges that the area covered by the covenant not to compete, and the nature and duration of the restrictions in this Section, are reasonable and necessary for the proper protection of BUYER. If any part of this Section is invalidated, the remainder of this Section will nevertheless continue to be valid and enforceable. If anyone successfully contests the validity or enforceability of this Section in its present form predicated upon the duration or area of coverage, this provision will not be deemed invalid or unenforceable, but will instead be deemed modified, so as to be valid and enforceable, to provide coverage for the maximum duration that any Court of competent jurisdiction will deem reasonable, necessary and equitable.

BUYER'S DUE DILIGENCE

BUYER, at BUYER's expense, shall be responsible for the initiation of any formal Due Diligence examination of the business operation and that that examination shall be conducted by the BUYER and/or by an appropriate professional. This Agreement shall be contingent upon the BUYER's satisfactory Due Diligence of the company's complete operations including, but not limited to, financial records, operational procedures, condition of equipment, any and all leases, and any contractual relationships. BUYER shall have _____ (___) days to complete the said Due Diligence. BUYER's Due Diligence Period shall commence on _____ ___, _____. BUYER's discovery, during the Due Diligence Period, of any item or items not to the BUYER's sole, complete and personal satisfaction shall cause this Agreement to be cancelled in every respect and particular. BUYER and SELLER agree that if this Agreement shall become cancelled because of the failure of Due Diligence, the Escrow Agent shall be vested with the authority to immediately refund any and all deposits held for this Agreement.

LEASE OF PREMISES

Within _____ (___) days prior to the date of Closing, SELLER shall execute an assignment for the lease on the Business premises with the Landlord's written consent. The BUYER shall assume the lease at Closing. This Agreement shall be subject to such consent where consent is required. Alternatively, at BUYER's option, SELLER shall assist BUYER, within the time constraints set out above, to obtain a new lease on substantially the same terms and conditions as the existing lease, to be effective as of the Closing Date.

CLOSING AGENT

The parties hereby appoint _____ as Closing Agent to receive, deposit and distribute funds for the parties as set forth in this Agreement. The parties agree that the Closing Agent shall prepare and obtain escrow instructions, closing documents and instruments evidencing the terms and conditions of this transaction as are required for the closing and conduct the closing and provide for recording of the documents. BUYER and SELLER agree to execute said documents as are reasonably requested by the Closing Agent and each is to pay one-half (1/2) of Closing Agent's fees and Closing Agent's expenses. The parties agree that the Closing Agent shall not be representing either SELLER or BUYER. All transferable taxes, insurance, licenses, rents, utilities and any other customarily prorated items shall be prorated as of the date of Closing.

INVENTORY

It is agreed that, included in the Purchase Price, the inventory at Closing of marketable goods at SELLER's cost shall be $_____. An itemized physical count of these goods held for resale shall be taken by BUYER and SELLER prior to the Closing and an increase or decrease as compared to this cost shall adjust the total purchase price. Where applicable, an increase shall be added to the Promissory Note owed to SELLER and a decrease shall reduce the cash down payment from BUYER.

ACCOUNTS RECEIVABLE

The accounts receivable of the Business for work done or goods sold prior to and including the date of Closing shall remain the property of SELLER. BUYER will forward to SELLER payments received by BUYER with respect to SELLER's Accounts Receivable and will cooperate with SELLER in providing all correspondence or other documents received by BUYER with respect to SELLER's Accounts Receivable and will otherwise cooperate with SELLER to enable SELLER to collect SELLER's Accounts Receivable.

PROMISSORY NOTE AND SECURITY AGREEMENT

At the time of Closing, BUYER shall execute in favor of the SELLER a Promissory Note as set forth in the Purchase Price above, personally guaranteed by the BUYER(s). BUYER shall execute a Security Agreement giving SELLER a lien against all assets purchased hereunder until the indebtedness is paid in full. Payment in full shall be due if any of the secured assets are sold to a third party other than in the ordinary course of business. The Security Agreement shall be subordinate to any existing liens described herein and shall contain the right of the SELLER to obtain, if the Note is in default, a court appointed receiver to preserve the business assets.

DEFAULT BY BUYER OR SELLER

If BUYER fails to pay the balance of any cash necessary to close this transaction,

or if the BUYER fails to perform
- any of the covenants and conditions of this Agreement, the SELLER shall have the right to enforce this Agreement pursuant to the Agreed terms.

If the SELLER shall default by failing to perform any of the covenants and conditions of this Agreement, BUYER shall
- have the right to terminate this Agreement, and demand the return of its escrow deposits, as well as reimbursement for any and all reasonable attorney's fees, accounting fees, and other costs incidental to BUYER's inspection of the business regardless of whether SELLER or BUYER should default.

If the SELLER shall default by failing to perform any of the covenants and conditions of this Agreement, BUYER may
- avail itself of any judicial remedy in law or in equity including specific performance.

FURTHER COOPERATION

Each of the parties agrees to take whatever actions as may be necessary to carry out the terms of this Agreement following the closing.

SURVIVAL OF REPRESENTATIONS

All representations, warranties and agreements of the parties contained in this Agreement shall survive the closing.

ATTORNEYS' FEES

In the event any party shall be forced to retain the services of legal counsel to enforce the terms of this Agreement whether suit be brought or not, the prevailing party shall be entitled to be reimbursed for all attorneys' fees and court costs incurred.

THIS IS A SAMPLE ASSET PURCHASE AGREEMENT FOR EDUCATIONAL PURPOSES ONLY. IT IS NOT TO BE USED FOR AN ACTUAL PURCHASE AND SALE AGREEMENT.

Buyer: _____ Seller: _____

_____ _____
Signature Signature

Dated: _____ Dated: _____

Brag Letter

Office of William Thomas
Address
City, State Zip

Special Announcement!

A WPB Window and Door Company Just Sold for 95% of Asking Price Plus a Generous 6 Month Compensation Package for the Sellers!

Owner
Business Name
Business Address
City, State Zip

Dear Owner,

My team and I can help *Sell Your Business* for MAXIMUM VALUE!

While financing was being arranged for the window and door company, our phone rang with buyers looking to purchase a window and door contractor. If you have ever thought of selling, now might be a fantastic time to do so.

If you are not interested in selling at this time but are wondering how much your business might be worth, feel free to give me a call and I will be happy to discuss it with you.

My skills as an experienced business broker allow me to analyze a business from a buyer's point of view and structure a deal prior to marketing your business. **So, my client's businesses sell for more money in less time!**

Please feel free to call me at **561-XXX-XXXX.**

Sincerely,

William Thomas
President, Florida Business Brokers
Specializing in the sale of privately held businesses with sales over $1 Million dollars.

p.s. Please read the comments on the back of this letter that come from clients who I've personally helped get TOP DOLLAR for their businesses.